Kant Machine

Political Theory and Contemporary Philosophy

Political Theory and Contemporary Philosophy encourages a sustained dialogue between the most important intellectual currents in recent European philosophy—including phenomenology, deconstruction, hermeneutics—and key political theories and concepts, both classical and modern. In doing so, it not only sheds new light on today's shifting political realities but also explores the previously neglected consequences of the two disciplines.

Series editor: Michael Marder and Giovanbattista Tusa

Other volumes in the series include:

Ethics under Capital: MacIntyre, Communication, and the Culture Wars, Jason Hannan

Politics in the Times of Indignation: The Crisis of Representative Democracy, Daniel Innerarity (translated by Sandra Kingery)

Medialogies: Inflationary Media and the Crisis of Reality, David R. Castillo and William Egginton

Democracy and Its Others, Jeffrey H. Epstein The Democracy of Knowledge, Daniel Innerarity (translated by Sandra Kingery)

The Voice of Conscience: A Political Genealogy of Western Ethical Experience, Mika Ojakangas

The Politics of Nihilism, edited by Nitzan Lebovic and Roy Ben-Shai

On Hegel's Philosophy of Right, Martin Heidegger (edited by Peter Trawny, Marcia Sá Cavalcante Schuback and Michael Marder, translated by Andrew J. Mitchell)

Deconstructing Zionism, Michael Marder and Santiago Zabala

Heidegger on Hegel's Philosophy of Right, Marcia Sá Cavalcante Schuback, Michael Marder and Peter Trawny

The Metaphysics of Terror, Rasmus Ugilt

The Negative Revolution, Artemy Magun

The Voice of Conscience, Mika Ojakangas

Contemporary Democracy and the Sacred, Jon Wittrock

The Fascism of Ambiguity, Marcia Sá Cavalcante Schuback

The Temptation of Non-Being, Artemy Magun

The Militant Philosopher, Andrey Gordienko

Kant Machine

Critical Philosophy after AI

Yuk Hui

BLOOMSBURY ACADEMIC
LONDON • NEW YORK • OXFORD • NEW DELHI • SYDNEY

BLOOMSBURY ACADEMIC
Bloomsbury Publishing Plc, 50 Bedford Square, London, WC1B 3DP, UK
Bloomsbury Publishing Inc, 1359 Broadway, New York, NY 10018, USA
Bloomsbury Publishing Ireland, 29 Earlsfort Terrace, Dublin 2, D02 AY28, Ireland

BLOOMSBURY, BLOOMSBURY ACADEMIC and the Diana logo are trademarks of
Bloomsbury Publishing Plc

First published in Great Britain 2026
Reprinted 2026

Copyright © Yuk Hui, 2026

Yuk Hui has asserted his right under the Copyright, Designs and Patents Act, 1988,
to be identified as Author of this work.

Series design by Jade Barnett
Cover images: Anson_iStock / Getty Images (robot hand), Europeana (Kant portrait)

All rights reserved. No part of this publication may be: i) reproduced or transmitted in any form, electronic or mechanical, including photocopying, recording or by means of any information storage or retrieval system without prior permission in writing from the publishers; or ii) used or reproduced in any way for the training, development or operation of artificial intelligence (AI) technologies, including generative AI technologies. The rights holders expressly reserve this publication from the text and data mining exception as per Article 4(3) of the Digital Single Market Directive (EU) 2019/790.

Bloomsbury Publishing Plc does not have any control over, or responsibility for, any third-party websites referred to or in this book. All internet addresses given in this book were correct at the time of going to press. The author and publisher regret any inconvenience caused if addresses have changed or sites have ceased to exist, but can accept no responsibility for any such changes.

A catalogue record for this book is available from the British Library.

A catalog record for this book is available from the Library of Congress.

ISBN: HB: 978-1-3505-6320-9
PB: 978-1-3506-0250-2
ePDF: 978-1-3505-6321-6
eBook: 978-1-3505-6322-3

Series: Political Theory and Contemporary Philosophy

Typeset by Deanta Global Publishing Services, Chennai, India
Printed and bound in Great Britain

For product safety related questions contact productsafety@bloomsbury.com.

To find out more about our authors and books visit www.bloomsbury.com and
sign up for our newsletters.

*For my grandmother, in memory
and for all that springs anew*

Can a machine be made to be super-critical?

– Alan Turing,
'Computing Machinery and Intelligence'

one can learn only mathematics, but never philosophy . . . at most one can only learn how to philosophize.

– Immanuel Kant, *Critique of Pure Reason*

Contents

Preface		viii
1	Intelligent machine: What kinds of machines are intelligent?	1
	§1. Cartesian machine versus Humean machine	2
	§2. Genesis of the Kantian machine	13
	§3. Kant among the cyberneticians	28
2	Moral machine: Are machines capable of being moral?	39
	§4. AI alignment and moral norms	45
	§5. Kantian moral machine	51
	§6. The moral, the teleological and the technological	67
3	Peace machine: Does an algorithm of perpetual peace exist?	75
	§7. Conflict of the universals	78
	§8. Algorithm of perpetual peace	89
	§9. Islands, shores and ships	100
Bibliography		109
Index		117

Preface

This work doesn't pretend to contribute to the already rich Kantian exegesis, well established over the past two hundred years; its humble aim is to seek Kantian inspiration so as to think about artificial intelligence: to resituate Kant's critical philosophy in the epoch of generative AI. The title of the book, *Kant Machine*, could be interpreted as both *Kant and Machines* or *Kantian Machines*, namely, Kant's critique of machines and machines endowed with Kantian motives. The starting point of this book is based on the following two claims:

1) Kant's philosophy could be read as a reflection on machines, or more precisely, on two ways of constructing machines, represented by rationalism and empiricism (which also imply dogmatism and scepticism). These two dominating schools of thought of the eighteenth century still occupy a central role in understanding machines today, exhibited by the debate between symbolism and connectionism.
2) Kant's philosophy, thus read in opposition to the machines of his time (which we refer to here as the Cartesian machine and the Humean machine), demonstrates a non-machinic thinking, which, paradoxically, could also be assimilated into a new form of machinic thought, or a 'mechano-organicism', a term I assigned to Hegel's dialectics and cybernetics.

Claims (1) and (2) are two sides of the same coin. What they share is both an ontological critique and an epistemological critique. The ontological critique rests on the irreducibility between machine and organism in the eighteenth century, that is, a living being cannot be reduced to a mechanical being governed by the laws of physics. The epistemological criticism is based on the understanding that linear causality, as one finds in mechanical beings, is insufficient; one should extrapolate a new kind of causality exhibited in living beings. Kant's contribution to epistemology, that is, the limit of the natural sciences, is significant, and its importance has been widely recognized by philosophers and historians. Yet what concerns the epistemological foundations in Kant's philosophy is no less important and it forms the central concern of the present work.

The influence of the epistemology of natural sciences on Kant's new way of philosophizing is something very crucial for understanding the evolution of his critical philosophy. In other words, one finds an epistemological foundation or, rather, several epistemological foundations underlying Kant's work. Some authors identify a physical foundation; for example, Jules Vuillemin reconnects Kantian philosophy of knowledge with his theory of physics;[1] Hermann Cohen reads Kant's theoretical philosophy as being shaped by Newtonian physics;[2] Hans Saner holds the same view that Kant's political philosophy was already informed by his second dissertation *Monadologia Physica* (1756), where Kant developed a dynamic concept of matter,[3] and that this influence lasted until Kant's later political writings such as 'Toward Perpetual Peace (1795)'.

As we know, Kant's 1770 *Inaugural Dissertation*, which returns to the distinction between the sensible world and the intelligent world, marks the beginning of his critical philosophy, as well as the adventure of reason.[4] Reason has the imperative to expand into realms in which no scientific knowledge is possible, like a ship departing from the shore of an island in a marine fog. Kant was inspired by research in biology (which, as a discipline, didn't yet exist), and the concept of epigenesis was central to Kant's three *Critique* and beyond. The writings of Philippe Huneman, John Zammito, Jennifer Mensch, Timothy Lenoir and others shed light on this epistemological foundation. In particular, Lenoir's *The Strategy of Life* reads nineteenth-century German biology as an elaboration on Kant's philosophical conceptualization of organism, which Lenoir calls a 'teleo-mechanist approach'.[5] Kant's three *Critiques* could be read as an elaboration on the epigenesis of reason, fluctuating between metaphysical and biological senses. It is primarily in the *Critique of Judgment* that the concept of reflective judgement (which was virtually absent in the first two *Critiques*) was more fully elaborated, and there we find a non-physical model, which we could describe in terms of an organic structure and a reflective (or better, recursive) operation.[6]

---

[1] Jules Vuillemin, *Physique et métaphysique kantiennes* (Paris: PUF, 1987).
[2] Hermann Cohen, *Kants Theorie der Erfahrung* (Berlin: Ferd. Dümmlers, 1885).
[3] Hans Saner, *Kant's Political Thought: Its Origin and Development* (Chicago, IL: The University of Chicago Press, 1973), 7.
[4] One could trace to even earlier work such as *Dreams of a Spirit-seer elucidated by Dreams of Metaphysics* (1766), however, the noumenon and phenomenon distinction is only explicit in the 1770 *Inaugural Dissertation*. The influence of his correspondence with Johann Heinrich Lambert on Kant's development is also clear and deserves our attention; see Harold Griffing, 'J. H. Lambert: A Study in the Development of the Critical Philosophy', *The Philosophical Review* 2, no. 1 (1893): 54–62.
[5] Timothy Lenoir, *The Strategy of Life* (Dordrecht: D. Reidel, 1982), 13.
[6] On this point, we will have to consider John Zammito's question, namely, 'why did teleology intrude' after the *Critique of Practical Reason* (1787)?; see John Zammito, *The Genesis of Kant's Critique of Judgment* (Chicago, IL: The University of Chicago Press, 1992), 2. However, deviating from Zammito's analysis, which brought Herder to the centre of Kant's third critique as the target of Kant's persistent attack (10), we prefer to understand it as an elaboration on the structure and operation of the 'systematic unity' of reason, which Kant couldn't satisfactorily answer in the first two *Critiques*.

This shift in epistemological foundation is our Ariadne's thread to trace the concept of machine in Kant and to understand Kant's philosophy as both an antidote to machines and partially a theory for future machines. This paradoxical movement, namely, the negation of mechanism leading to a teleomechanism (as Lenoir terms it), a teleonomy (as Ernst Mayr calls it), a mechano-organicism (as we call it) or some other formulations, is crucial for locating Kant's critical philosophy in our contemporary scientific landscape.[7] Gerhard Lehmann in an article 'Technik der Natur' claims that Kant's theory of teleology in the third *Critique* is supplemented by his *Nachlass* (*Ak.* 21/22) in formulating a philosophy of technology or a critique of technological reason.[8] Lehmann's commentary on Kant has been recently rediscovered and systematically elaborated in Franziska Aigner's *Kant and Technics*,[9] one of the rare and important treatises defending a philosophy of technology in Kant. However, we would like to show: first, that Lehmann's critique against mechanism and its subordination to a higher realm of 'technics of nature' seems to be overcome, or *at least* challenged by contemporary technologies, especially after the rise of cybernetics; therefore, if there is a critique of technological reason in Kant, Lehmann's discovery deserves a new interpretation and evaluation; second, that the concept of technics in the 'technics of nature' could only be *concretely* comprehended when we have the cybernetic machine or artificial intelligence in mind; otherwise, it would only be *analogically* understood in relation to the aesthetic judgement of an artwork (and not art making).

To reiterate, our key question is: How relevant is Kant's critical philosophy to our reflection on contemporary machines, especially artificial intelligence and machine learning? It occurs to me that the current debates are repetitions of the background that gave rise to Kant's critical philosophy. Precisely for this reason, Kant is more than relevant to our understanding of contemporary machines. Although undeniably, machines are *becoming* organic, as Gilbert Simondon

---

[7] This is evident in Kant's letter to Blumenbach (5 August 1790) where he writes 'I wish to extend my thanks for sending me last year your excellent work on the formative force [*Bildungstrieb*]. I have learned a great deal from your writings. Indeed, in your new work, you unite two principles – the physical-mechanical and the sheerly teleological mode of explanation of organized nature. These are modes which one would not have thought capable of being united. In this you have quite closely approached the idea with which I have been chiefly occupied – but an idea that required such confirmation [as you provide] through facts', see Immanuel Kant, *Briefwechsel*, ed. Otto Schöndörffer (Hamburg: Felix Meiner Verlag, 1972), 466; also quoted by Robert J. Richards, 'Kant and Blumenbach on the *Bildungstrieb*: A Historical Misunderstanding', *Studies in History and Philosophy of Biological and Biomedical Sciences* 31, no. 1 (2000): 11–32.

[8] Gerhard Lehmann, 'Technik der Natur', in *Beiträge zur Geschichte und Interpretation der Philosophie Kants* (Berlin: De Gruyter, 1969), 294.

[9] Franziska Aigner, *Kant and Technics: From the Critique of Pure Reason to the Opus Postumum* (London: Bloomsbury, 2024).

observed in 1958 in light of the development of cybernetics; it, however, doesn't imply that they *are* organic. In relation to Kant, Simondon made an intriguing statement in an article titled 'Epistemology of Cybernetics (1953)', that 'Kant could only deal with cybernetics by situating it in the *Critique of Judgment*'.[10] This remark is of extreme importance for us, since if we want to understand the place of cybernetics in the history of philosophy, we will need to understand Kant; and if we would like to understand Kant's relevance to contemporary technology, we will need to appreciate the significance of cybernetics.[11] In other words, Kant is essential for the study of the relation between philosophy and machines, as well as for appreciating their intimacy, which Kant himself didn't anticipate, and which we only know retrospectively. From the 1950s until now, technical concretization has far exceeded Simondon's imagination; contemporary AI, robotics, bioinformatics, among other new technologies, have brought significant challenges to philosophical studies, and philosophy will have to respond to these challenges not with mere resistance, but rather to understand their limits and at the same time render these challenges in service of reason, like what Kant did to the natural sciences, especially Newtonian physics. In this sense, it is also the moment to reposition critical philosophy in this new historical context by reading Kant in parallel with Turing, Gödel, Wiener, Solomonoff, Minsky, McCarthy, Newell, Hinton, Bengio, LeCun, among many other pioneers in AI.

In order to present this project more efficiently, and to avoid getting drowned in the huge reservoir of Kant scholarship, we will mainly place these scholarly references in the footnotes, thereby keeping the main text concise. The footnotes dialogue with the main text, enabling the reader to extend their own exploration of Kant and his commentators. The main text will hence focus on Kant's own writings, highlighting the question of the machine as it appears. We thus orient the current work around three major questions:

1) What could be called an intelligent machine?
2) Are machines capable of being moral?
3) Does an algorithm of perpetual peace exist?

---

[10] Gilbert Simondon, *Sur la Philosophie* (Paris: PUF, 2016), 180, 'Kant n'aurait pu traiter de la Cybernétique qu'en la situant dans la *Critique du jugement*'.

[11] This doesn't mean that Simondon accepts Kant as the philosopher of modern science and technology; indeed, Simondon is very critical of him, as we can read in the Kant entry in his 'History of the Individual', 'A critique of knowledge like the one Kant produced could no longer apply to the world of electromagnetism or thermodynamics, for the field or the law of the increase in entropy are not only a way to connect phenomena, but also the very weft of phenomena, their manner of being, and more than their condition of appearing', see Gilbert Simondon, *Individuation in the Light of the Notions of Form and Information* (Minneapolis, MN: University of Minnesota Press, 2021), 630. This remark, as Joel White reminded me, is sharp and controversial; one will need to interpret what he said, but it is not the task of this work.

Readers might immediately find resonances with Kant's three famous questions: 'what can I know', 'what must I do' and 'what may I hope for', though these questions are transposed from humans to machines, from the organic to the inorganic; therefore, the latent question would be 'what is machine?' instead of 'what is human?' The first question examines the concept of 'intelligence' by investigating critical philosophy's criticism of dogmatism and scepticism and its grounding of the transcendental faculties. The second question examines the concept of 'morality' by reflecting on Kant's criticism that in Jacques de Vaucanson's automaton, the question of freedom is unthinkable, and also asking if contemporary machines can become moral machines once the antagonistic relation between autonomy and automation is subject to critical reexamination. The third question examines the concept of perpetual peace by re-reading Kant's late writings on politics (1791–8). Kant, as we know, had already decided at the age of forty to stay in Königsberg forever, being described as a boring man who repeated the same promenade every day; however, the old Kant, as Ernst Cassirer reported, considered leaving Königsberg because of the censorship against him on his writings on religion, and he was thus ready to give up both lecturing philosophy and his *Heimat*.[12] The late Kant's political writing is extraordinary since Kant, not being a supporter of the revolution while being a defender of philosophy, or more precisely, reason, had to identify a new form of political struggle as a dissident. These writings are implications of Kant's critical philosophy in confrontation with concrete social and political problems; they contain some of Kant's profound reflections on the strategies of *resistance*; and in this spirit, we are tempted to read his 'Toward Perpetual Peace' as the proposal of an algorithm for perpetual peace based on international trade.

These three questions allow us to re-read Kant among the machines. They are also fundamental to my trilogy, that is, *Recursivity and Contingency* (2019), *Art and Cosmotechnics* (2021) and *Machine and Sovereignty* (2024), in which Kant's philosophy serves as the departure point of the reflections on metaphysics, aesthetics and politics. This work puts Kant at the centre of the discussion, building on and extending various threads from my previous studies on his thought, attempting to offer a more systematic view of my interpretation of Kant as well as a concluding note to a long process of studying Kant. Therefore, I decided to refrain from developing the implication of my reading of Kant

---

[12] Ernst Cassirer, *Kant's Life and Thought*, trans. James Haden (New Haven, CT: Yale University Press, 1983), 394.

(which was discussed in the above-mentioned monographs, though yet to be exhausted), and only limit this book to elucidating Kant's thoughts and their relevance to contemporary reflections on machines. I hope this book can be inspiring to philosophers who want to engage with AI and the history of philosophy beyond analytic philosophy and cognitive science; it is not my intention to depreciate them, since they remain essential for understanding the operation of AI, and indeed without which, one might commit another kind of illusion by using non-logical schema to capture logical schema. However, in the Kantian spirit, we should always bear in mind the epigenesis of reason and the desire for wisdom. Philosophy as a doctrine of wisdom constantly searches for truth and defends reason, and reason must be expanded under critical conditions. I hope this book can be equally appealing to engineers who would like to understand the background and complexity of the philosophical questions that they are dealing with, as well as to readers who are curious about philosophy and technology.

This book wouldn't be possible without the support of many colleagues and friends. I would like to thank Howard Caygill, whose Kantian inspirations have had a longstanding effect on me over the past decade, and to whom once I promised a book on Kant during his visit to Lüneburg in 2016. I would equally want to thank colleagues who have either engaged in discussions about this project or commented on the manuscript, including Bryon Norton, Warren Sack, Joel White, Hub Zwart, Susanna Lindberg, Mario García Pascual, Pieter Lemmens, Marie Louise Krogh, Franziska Aigner, Kohei Ise and Milan Stürmer. I shouldn't forget to express my gratitude to Nicholas Walker, with whom I studied German when I was a student at Goldsmiths College, for being a model of scholarship in German philosophy and literature. Lastly, I want to thank the two anonymous reviewers for their endorsement of this project, Michael Marder and Giovanni Tusa for accepting this book in their series.

Yuk Hui
Rotterdam/New York
Summer 2025

The references to Kant's work (cited *Ak.*) follow Kant's *Gesammelte Schriften. Ausgabe der Preußischen (later Deutschen) Akademie der Wissenschaften* (Berlin Georg Reimer, later Walter de Gruyter, 1902–).

The English translation of the first two *Critiques* follows that of Werner S. Pluhar, and the third *Critique* follows the translation from James Creed Meredith with revision by Nicholas Walker.

1

Intelligent machine

What kinds of machines are intelligent?

In his lecture on ACE (Automatic Computing Engine) at the Royal Academy of Science in 1947, Alan Turing attempted to defend the existence of machine intelligence. Turing questions the stereotype, which often sees machines as inferior slaves, and which doesn't treat them in a fair manner. Turing rejects that such a stereotype could be valid at all, for machines evolve over time. Turing sees storage as a crucial part to this evolutionary process. Machines in the past had limited storage, but the situation has, of late, been changing.[1] Ada Lovelace's famous claim, quoted elsewhere by Turing, that 'The Analytical Engine has no pretensions to *originate* anything. It can do whatever *we know how to order it* to perform' is only valid according to the machines of her time, the mid-nineteenth century; however, it certainly does not imply that machines will forever remain as stated.[2] It is possible to imagine that machines – here Turing refers to machines built upon ACE which possess a large amount of storage[3] – might exhibit intelligence, namely a machine that does not simply follow rules but is also capable of learning:

> In such a case one would have to admit that the progress of the machine had not been foreseen when its original instructions were put in. It would be like a pupil who had learnt much from his master, but had added much more by his own work. When this happens I feel that one is obliged to regard the machine

---

[1] Turing's more systematic arguments for machine intelligence are to be found in his 'Intelligent Machinery: A Report by A. M. Turing' (1948) and 'Computing Machinery and Intelligence' (1950), in *The Essential Turing: Seminal Writings in Computing, Logic, Philosophy, Artificial Intelligence, and Artificial Life: Plus The Secrets of Enigma*, ed. B. Jack Copeland (Oxford: Clarendon Press, 2004), 410–464.
[2] Turing, 'Computing Machinery and Intelligence', 455.
[3] In comparison to speed, Turing considers storage a more fundamental element of the computational machine.

as showing intelligence. As soon as one can provide a reasonably large memory capacity it should be possible to begin to experiment on these lines.[4]

For Turing, a machine that merely executes instructions is not yet intelligent; what is most important is that 'it can learn from experience'.[5] Therefore, Turing proposes that if one can simulate a child's mind, then it will be possible to develop that mind into an adult's mind through learning.[6] The intelligent machine here defined by Turing is an empirical machine, and intelligence would be measured according to the knowledge acquired from experience. In response to Lovelace's criticism of machines, Turing asks if a machine can be 'super-critical' in the sense that it will not be limited to an idea 'injected' into it; instead, it can produce and reproduce more ideas.[7] If we follow Turing in considering AI as an empirical machine, the question remains: What exactly is this intelligence that can render empirical experience useful to itself? In the case of Turing, it is clear that computational machinery was built according to different faculties, for example, memory, control, arithmetic logic unit and input/output.[8] What kind of organization makes it intelligent? What is the essence of this kind of organization? These are questions crucial for understanding the status of machines today, for example, nativism versus empiricism, but to answer them, we have to, first, go back to the history before Turing.[9]

§1. Cartesian machine versus Humean machine

Then, where to start? This brings us to a question already raised by Allen Newell in his 1982 article 'Intellectual Issues in the History of Artificial Intelligence',

---

[4] Turing, 'Lecture on the Automatic Computing Engine (1947)', in *The Essential Turing*, 393.
[5] Turing, 'Lecture on the Automatic Computing Engine', 393.
[6] Turing, 'Computing Machinery and Intelligence', 460.
[7] Turing, 'Computing Machinery and Intelligence', 459, 'An idea presented to such a mind may give rise to a whole "theory" consisting of secondary, tertiary and more remote ideas. Animals minds seem to be very definitely sub-critical. Adhering to this analogy we ask, "Can a machine be made to be super-critical?"'
[8] Turing, 'Lecture on the Automatic Computing Engine', 384.
[9] These questions were debated already in two or even three centuries before Turing, though they still stay with us today. In 2017, David Chalmers organized a debate between Yann LeCun and Gary Marcus at the NYU, see https://www.youtube.com/watch?v=vdWPQ6iAkT4. The debate could be summarized as a confrontation between nativism (Marcus) versus empiricism (LeCun), where Marcus claims that his view is a continuation of Plato and Kant. In cognitive science, nativism holds the view that certain cognitive structures, abilities or knowledge are innate rather than acquired through experience; we can identify some well-known nativist claims such as Noam Chomsky's universal grammar, Jerry Fodor's modularity of mind (i.e. domain-specific modules), Steven Pinker's language instinct (i.e. language is a gene determined development), Elizabeth Spelke's core knowledge theory (i.e. infants are born with innate fundamental knowledge).

namely, 'How is the history of artificial intelligence to be written?' Provided that AI was and is still in its early stage, theoretical frameworks such as Thomas Kuhn's paradigm shift cannot yet be applied, since there was hardly a paradigm at all.[10] However, does AI really have as short a history as Newell argued (we are told that it was established around 1955, and officially announced during the Dartmouth conference that took place in 1956)? One could, at least, respond with certainty that there have already been long histories concerning the discourse on intelligence – and by putting history in its plural form we want to emphasize that there is no single historical discourse on intelligence in view of diverse cultures and ways of thinking. We can indeed locate the place of artificial intelligence in the history of Western philosophy. It is possible to study the similarity between the history of artificial intelligence and the history of early modern philosophy as a *transposition* of the philosophical problems regarding human cognition to the machine. In other words, returning to the history of philosophy might allow us to shed light on any hidden areas in the contemporary debates or the complications of the subject matter thus far ignored. In an article by the AI scientists Jacob Browning and Yann LeCun published in 2022, we can read:

> At the heart of this debate are two different visions of the role of symbols in intelligence, both biological and mechanical: One holds that symbolic reasoning must be hard-coded from the outset and the other holds it can be learned through experience, by machines and humans alike.[11]

'Hard coded' refers to operations based on pregiven 'rational' rules, and 'learning from experience' refers to empirical associations. The concept of intelligence framed as such is either limited to rationalism or empiricism – the two schools, as it is often described by textbooks in the history of philosophy, which Kant set to overcome. Here, we take this established history strategically so as to expose the similarity of the problems concerning intelligence that we are dealing with today. In rationalism, we see that intelligence is defined by the operation of logical inferences which exclude the irrational from entering into the reasoning process. Thinking is conceived to be a process that is regulated by formal and logical rules, according to which the world is ordered, and its existence is justified; certainly, one can have fantasies and dreams, but they are the source of errors because truth presupposes rationality. This form of intelligence belongs to what we might call the Cartesian machine. The Cartesian machine is one which

---

[10] Allen Newell, 'Intellectual Issues in the History of Artificial Intelligence (1982)', in *The study of information: interdisciplinary messages September*, ed. Fritz Machlup and Una Mansfield (New York: John Wiley & Son, 1983), 187-227, 188.
[11] Jacob Browning and Yann LeCun, 'What AI Can Tell Us About Intelligence', *Noema*, 2022, https://www.noemamag.com/what-ai-can-tell-us-about-intelligence/.

first seeks an axiom capable of resisting the manipulations of the infamous malicious demon [*malin genie*] – a demon Descartes imagined at the beginning of the *Meditations*, where he asks whether the world that appears to us is nothing more than illusions produced by such a demon. Descartes, instead of accepting the existence of the world, including the sky, the mountains, trees and houses, which are often regarded as true existence, assumes that they could be illusions and therefore couldn't be the foundation of knowledge. However, he is able to put aside all experience enthralled by things existing outside of him, in order to arrive at an axiom concerning the 'I think', which cannot be doubted and that serves as the beginning of a thinking process as well as a knowledge system guided by *clarity* and *distinctness*.

This rationalism resonates with mechanism, and indeed they march hand in hand. The machine gives Descartes an archetype of rationality, like form in Aristotelian hylomorphism, which is applicable everywhere, ranging from perception, sensation and other corporeal operations. There is an analogy between the animal and the machine, the body and the clock – the Cartesian machine par excellence; this does not necessarily mean that an animal *is* a machine, but that how the animal functions could be explained by the same mechanical principles that govern a clock, or a church organ. For example, when Descartes talks about human sense-perception, he claims that it 'occurs in the same way in which wax takes on an impression from a seal', but it shouldn't be thought that he has 'a mere analogy in mind'.[12] Similarly, in his essay titled 'Description of the Human Body (1662)', he compares the human body to a church organ, likening the heart to a pump, blood vessels to pipes and animal spirits to wind.[13] In Descartes, mechanism and rationalism join together because of their common share of geometrical reason. Since the latter is that which could effectively exclude error, as Descartes writes in the *Discourse*:

> Those long chains composed of very simple and easy reasonings, which geometers customarily use to arrive at their most difficult demonstrations, had given me occasion to suppose that all the things which can fall under human knowledge are interconnected in the same way. And I thought that, provided we refrain from accepting anything as true which is not, and always keep to the order required for deducing one thing from another, there can be nothing too remote to be reached in the end or too well hidden to be discovered.[14]

---

[12] René Descartes, 'Rules for the Direction of the Mind', Rules XII, in *The Philosophical Writings of Descartes Vol. 1* (Cambridge: Cambridge University Press, 1985), 41.
[13] Descartes, 'Description of the Human Body', in *The Philosophical Writings Vol. 1*, 322–3.
[14] Descartes, 'Discourse on the Method', in *The Philosophical Writings Vol. 1*, 120.

Much more could be said about Descartes's animal-machine,[15] however, here, what we intend to point out is that mechanism was presented as an epistemology through which the animal and the machine were governed by the same deductive model of reasoning. This mechanism is based on a linear causality assured by the necessity between a prior cause and a posterior effect. This way of understanding intelligence, typical of the seventeenth century, didn't disappear; instead, it was resurrected during the early days of artificial intelligence. According to history of artificial intelligence, it starts with what is known as symbolic AI, a formal logical representation of meanings and objects. However, symbolic representation remains only an assumption since no one has yet been able to demonstrate the nature of intelligence in general; such assumptions thus remain hypothetical. This was affirmed as such by Marvin Minsky in his 'Steps Toward Artificial Intelligence' (1961) that 'There is, of course, no generally accepted theory of "intelligence"; the analysis is our own and may be controversial'.[16] Later, this assumption that intelligence starts with the cognitive representation of the world was challenged. The presupposition of the undoubtful in the beginning and the step-by-step seeking of the goal through logical inferences limit not only the action of the agent but also the way the world should be perceived. The world is more complex than any codification of the cognitive schema. This difficulty is identified in what John Haugland calls the 'paradox of mechanisation', or put it in his own words: 'If a process or system is mechanical, it can't reason; if it reasons, it can't be mechanical'.[17] Reasoning means first of all understanding meanings, while if a mechanical system treats everything as symbols, then it doesn't really understand the meaning of both these symbols and what is represented by these symbols. Rationalism, in its *mechanical form*, cannot adequately explain intelligence. This is also why Hubert Dreyfus was able to call the early AI, now known as Good Old-Fashioned AI (named by John Haugland[18]), Cartesian AI. The Cartesian AI is one in which the agent is the subject that attempts to describe the world from the perspective of the subject; everything is seen as what Heidegger calls present-at-hand [*Vorhandenheit*], namely it is a bearer of properties; it is objectified by the subject according to logical forms intrinsic

---

[15] For a detailed account of mechanism in Descartes's philosophy, see Yuk Hui, *Recursivity and Contingency* (London: Rowman and Littlefield, 2019), Chapter 3 'The Organized Inorganic' and Jessica Riskin, *The Restless Clock* (Chicago, IL: The University of Chicago Press, 2016), Chapter 2 'Descartes Among the Machines'.
[16] Marvin Minsky, 'Steps toward Artificial Intelligence', *Proceedings of the IRE* 49, no. 1 (January 1961): 8–30, 9.
[17] John Haugland, *Artificial Intelligence: The Very Idea* (Cambridge, MA: MIT Press, 1989), 39.
[18] Hubert L. Dreyfus, *Skillful Coping: Essays on the Phenomenology of Everyday Perception and Action*, ed. Mark Wrathall (Oxford: Oxford University Press, 2014), 251.

in language or through cognitive schema of subjective explication, which Dreyfus retrospectively associates with Descartes and Husserl. Or perhaps we might even call it logical atomism, as seems to be the case in Terry Winograd's characterization:

> We are concerned with developing a formalism, or 'representation,' with which to describe ... knowledge. We seek the 'atoms' and 'particles' of which it is built, and the 'forces' that act on it.[19]

Dreyfus's mapping of AI development within the history of philosophy reveals that since the very beginning of philosophy, it has been a primary task to examine the nature of intelligence, and therefore, a return to the history of philosophy concerning intelligence could also anticipate the limits and the possibilities of artificial intelligence. As an affirmation of Minsky's claim that there is no monopoly on the definition of intelligence, Dreyfus showed further that all definitions of intelligence involve various presuppositions which could become problematic under examination, including Minsky's own definition:

> Even a chair is not understandable in terms of any set of facts or 'elements of knowledge.' To recognize an object as a chair, for example, means to understand its relation to other objects and to human beings. This involves a whole context of human activity of which the shape of our body, the institution of furniture, the inevitability of fatigue, constitute only a small part. In assuming that what is given are facts at all, Minsky is simply echoing a view which has been developing since Plato and has now become so ingrained as to seem self-evident.[20]

A counterexample to Minsky's theory of intelligence that Dreyfus discussed throughout his work is what Heidegger calls ready-to-hand [*Zuhandenheit*]: a thing in the world, such as a tool, cannot be merely thematized and isolated as an object, namely, objectively described as something standing against the subject as the German word for object *Gegenstand* literally means. Instead of being seen as a bearer of properties, the tool [*Zeug*] must be understood through its equipmentality [*Zeughaftigkeit*], characterized by its 'in-order-to' [*um-zu*] structure. This equipmentality implies a network of references [*Verweisungszusammenhang*] that we navigate seamlessly in daily life, allowing us

---

[19] Terry Winograd, 'Artificial Intelligence and Language Comprehension', in *Artificial Intelligence and Language Comprehension* (Washington, DC: National Institute of Education, 1976), 9; also cited by Dreyfus, *Skilful Coping*, 216.

[20] Hubert L. Dreyfus, *What Computers Cannot Do: A Critique of Artificial Reason* (New York: Harper & Row, 1972), 122–3.

to handle tools without the need for explicit objectification.[21] This phenomenon is often referred to as embodiment: the world is embodied within the subject, while simultaneously, the subject is embedded within the world. What is at play is not merely the immediate perception of the world but also a background network of references.[22] For example, when we open a door, we typically do not examine the properties of the doorknob or the door itself; rather, we engage with the door through an intuitive understanding of its place within a network of references already embodied in human Dasein. This network of references also defines what we might call spatiality, in contrast to space as homogeneous volume. It would be a mistake to merely analyse an object according to space, since its presence is a constellation of relations, which could only be apprehended as spatiality. A good example of spatiality, which Heidegger uses in *Being and Time*, would be when the power cuts at home and it results in complete darkness, one is still able to orient oneself according to the network of references remembered without being able to see the objects.[23] Heidegger's critique of the history of ontology reveals a 'non-cognitive precondition of all understanding' as Dreyfus quotes from Heidegger's *Being and Time*:

> [T]he 'in-order-to', the 'for-the-sake-of', and the 'with-which' of an involvement... resist any sort of mathematical functionalization; nor are they merely something thought, first posted in an 'act of thinking.' They are rather relationships in which concernful circumspection as such already dwells.[24]

In a nutshell, rationalism, thus defined, cannot explain human intelligence; it can, at most, provide us with a metaphysics which is analytic in nature, namely that truth is implied in the concept itself. Dreyfus's own work, as well as his co-authored work with his brother Stuart Dreyfus, leaves us rich resources to understand the intimate relation between continental philosophy and artificial intelligence. Dreyfus mobilized Heidegger's critique of Cartesianism and destruction of ontologies that presuppose the world as merely present-at-hand in *Being and Time* to challenge the Cartesian machine exemplified by the methodological approach of the early artificial intelligence research. Dreyfus turned continental philosophy into something useful for computer scientists – as

---

[21] Martin Heidegger, *Being and Time*, trans. John Macquarrie and Edward Robinson (New York: Harper & Row, 1962), §15, 97, 'Taken seriously, there "is" no such thing as *an* equipment. To the Being of any equipment there always belongs to a totality of equipment, in which it can be this equipment that it is. Equipment is essentialy "something in-order-to..."'
[22] See Heidegger, *Being and Time*, §17–18.
[23] See Heidegger, *Being and Time*, §23. 'The Spatiality of Being-in-the-world'.
[24] Heidegger, *Being and Time*, 122; also quoted by Dreyfus, *Skillful Coping*, 133.

we know, this privilege has been almost exclusively granted to analytic philosophy. Terry Winograd, Philip Agre[25] and a few others took Dreyfus's critique seriously and tried to understand its implications in the design of artificial intelligence. Notwithstanding his rigorous critique, Dreyfus, not being a computer scientist working on concrete projects, couldn't shed light on how a 'Heideggerian AI' would be realizable. On the other hand, were a Heideggerian AI possible, then it would also mean the defeat of Heideggerian philosophy, since the latter claims that thinking is irreducible to calculation [*Berechenbarkeit*]. Dreyfus hinted frequently at connectionism, a branch of research in AI promoted by Frank Rosenblatt.[26] Connectionism was quickly suppressed by symbolism.[27] Indeed, it is said that Marvin Minsky and Seymour Papert's 1969 book *Perceptrons: an Introduction to Computational Geometry* marked the beginning of a neural network winter. Connectionism returned to the stage towards the end of the 1970s after the failure of symbolic AI.[28] It is also considered the precursor to today's machine learning.[29] Symbolic AI, relying on a predefined formal representation of the world, is proved to be an inadequate understanding of intelligence.[30] Connectionism, or what is known more widely today as the neural network, is fundamental to the implementation of the learning process. A neural network consists of multiple layers of neurons; during training, the parameters

---

[25] Agre's book *Computation and Human Experience* (Cambridge: Cambridge University Press, 1997) shows not only the influence of Heidegger but also Derrida and others. Winograd has been teaching Heidegger's *Being and Time* in his AI classes, but as he admitted that his understanding of Heidegger is limited to Dreyfus' interpretation of division I of *Being and Time*, see Terry Winograd, 'LLM has a representation of care, it doesn't care. An interview with Terry Winograd by Harry Halpin,' *Technophany Commentaries* (2025), https://philotechne.substack.com/p/commentaries-llm-has-a-representation

[26] Dreyfus's interpretation was largely influenced by the work of Walter Freeman on neurodynamics. On another note, one might argue that Turing was the first who proposed a model of neural network, which he calls 'unorganized machine;' Turing also considers the cortex as an unorganized machine, see 'Intelligent Machinery', 416–8, 423–4.

[27] See Dreyfus, *Skillful Coping*, 210–3.

[28] It is marked by the Parallel Models of Associative Memory workshop that Geoffrey Hinton and James Anderson organized in La Jolla, California in 1979. For a more elaborated history on deep learning and the historical debates and conflicts between symbolism and connectionism, see Terrence J. Sejnowski, *The Deep learning Revolution* (Cambridge, MA: MIT Press, 2018). In the same book, Sejnowski recounted his question to Minsky during the 'Dartmouth Artificial Intelligence Conference: The Next Fifty Years' (July 13–15, 2006) if Minsky was the devil responsible for the neural network winter, and Minsky admitted (258).

[29] For a comprehensive outline of the history of machine learning not restricted to the popular discourses, but also different kinds of learning (e.g. supervised learning, unsupervised learning, reinforcement learning) see Jürgen Schmidhuber, 'Deep Learning in Neural Networks: An Overview', *Neural Networks* 61 (2015): 85–117.

[30] Descartes had to constantly review his mechanization of the human body in order to cope with the discrepancy that arises between the mechanical model and human experience, for example, the animal spirit, intellectual memory (as opposed to bodily memory) and so on, overall, memory stands out as a major technical issue which Turing shared with in his writing, as we have seen earlier in this chapter.

(or weights) associated with these neurons are updated based on the learning process, allowing each layer to gradually specialize in different aspects of the task (e.g. backpropagation algorithm).[31] This flexibility enables the development of systems capable of optimizing their internal parameters through learning, effectively adapting their behavior based on data rather than predefined rules. Connectionism, in its essence, is empiricism: the world is a collection of facts, and thinking means appropriate associations of facts according to principles. The lack of examination of empiricism in Dreyfus's critique of artificial intelligence is regrettable since it could have served as a self-critique of Dreyfus's own proposal regarding the realization of a so-called 'Heideggerian AI'.[32] Empiricism is foremost a scepticism against any truth claim which cannot be explained by experience. The concept of substance, for example, cannot be experienced, therefore, it should be contested. Causality is determined not by the logical assertion but rather by the frequency of occurrence in our experience.

Rationalism and empiricism are re-embedded in the development of computational machines. The triumph of empiricism today is largely due to the advancements in GPU technology which provides an increasingly lower cost of computational power, and the proliferation of sensors and mobile devices enables capturing huge amounts of data. These data sets are aggregates of empirical facts, which could be structured, organized and assembled so that a certain kind of 'consciousness' can arise. Though each school developed their own theory of consciousness, both rationalism and empiricism fail to explain intelligence. Indeed, one tends to conflate consciousness with intelligence; however, being conscious doesn't imply being intelligent. To be conscious is to be conscious of something, either the self or an external object. There is no intelligence without consciousness, however, consciousness alone cannot explain intelligence, which carries the meaning 'to understand', 'to discern'.[33] Traditional rationalism as a principle of intelligence was rejected in the history of AI after the rise of connectionism; empiricism became an alternative thinking power, or as we may call it: a Humean machine.[34] A Humean machine is more than just the inductive

---

[31] Yoshua Bengio, Yann LeCun, and Geoffrey Hinton, 'Deep Learning for AI', Turing Lecture 2021, Communications of the ACM, https://cacm.acm.org/research/deep-learning-for-ai/.

[32] Hubert Dreyfus, 'Why Heideggerian AI Failed and How Fixing it Would Require Making it More Heideggerian', *Artificial Intelligence* 171, no. 18 (2007): 1137–60.

[33] In the *Jäsche Logic*, Kant classifies seven degrees of cognition, where we see that consciousness (including presenting and cognizing) occupies a lower degree than intelligence (including to understand [*intelligere*], to cognize though reason [*perspicere*] and to comprehend [*comprehendere*]), see Immanuel Kant, *Lectures on Logic*, trans. J. Michael Young (Cambridge: Cambridge University Press, 1992), 299, Ak 9: 64–5.

[34] The term 'Humean machine' was inspired by Bruno Latour and G. Teil, 'The Hume Machine. Can Associations Networks Do More Than Formal Rules?' *Stanford Humanities Review* 4, no. 2 (1995): 47–66.

method mechanized, as one might be inclined to understand it. Instead, it is one which operates according to the rules of associations, namely resemblance, contiguity in time and space, and causality. Humean associationism is a pattern language which constantly searches for possibilities of association according to principles. In comparison with the Cartesian machine, which starts with an absolute 'I think' so that all logical developments can be assured, and that the world manipulated by the malicious demon can be ignored, the Humean machine starts with contingent experience and constantly develops itself according to the strength and degree of associations. In the Humean machine, instead of substance and concept, impressions and ideas reign. The source of impression and idea is 'matter of fact'; we can say that ideas are faded impressions, and they stay in our memory and re-emerge in our imagination. Impressions and ideas are associated according to relations: contiguity, resemblance and causality. The most famous controversial relation is causality. For a rationalist, causality means necessity; otherwise, there is no law to follow, and the world will be conquered by contingency, as Leibniz's principle of sufficient reason clearly demands that *nihil est sine ratione*; for an empiricist, the relation between cause and effect depends on constant conjunctions. In other words, the necessary connexion between a cause and an effect is determined first by contiguity (effect next to cause) and sequence (cause prior to effect), but most importantly by constant conjunction, namely the association between the cause and effect *doesn't discover and produce anything new*.[35] However, even though this necessary connection is guaranteed by the constant conjunction of the present and in memory, there is no guarantee that such a conjunction still holds in the next moment. In other words, this connection cannot be called necessary since it is not guaranteed. When Judea Pearl criticized that the current form of AI doesn't yet know what causality is,[36] it is not that it doesn't know, but rather that such a concept of causality has no meaning other than the frequency and probability of occurrence, namely what is important is correlation but not the rationalist concept of causality.

In short, the Humean machine is a machine that functions according to relations defined by contiguity, resemblance and causality. Today, it is most apparent that if we were to consider the recommender algorithm of many platforms then what is recommended is calculated according to parameters such

---

[35] David Hume, *A Treatise of Human Nature Vol. 1 Text* (Oxford: Clarendon Press, 2007), 1.3.14.
[36] See Judea Pearl and Dana McKenzie, *The Book of Why: The New Science of Cause and Effect* (New York: Basic Books, 2018), 10, 'machines' lack of understanding of causal relations' as being 'perhaps the biggest roadblock to giving them human-level intelligence [. . .] I believe that strong AI is an achievable goal and one not to be feared precisely because causality is part of the solution'.

as your contextual information, for example, location and time (contiguity), your preferences (resemblance) and the habits you exhibited on the platform (causality). Hume's doctrine of associationism basically dissolved substance into relations, and by doing so, he also prioritizes intensity and duration as the criteria for truth. Some contemporary philosophers, inspired by process philosophy and a certain reading of Deleuze, have criticized that Western philosophy prioritizes substance over relation, however, one should also be aware that Hume was a veritable thinker of relations, and he indeed refused the concept of substance, for no one has an impression of substance, therefore it cannot exist. Contiguity, resemblance and causality are three kinds of relations Hume calls in *A Treatise of Human Nature* 'natural relations', but Hume doesn't find them adequate and in the same book, he proposes seven kinds of 'philosophical relations': resemblance, identity, space and time, quantity, quality, contrariety and causality.[37] In other words, we can say that Hume abandoned the fetish of substance philosophy inherited from Aristotle and relaunched a philosophy of relations subsequent to the theological attempt of the scholastics.[38]

One might contest that the current artificial intelligence or machine learning algorithms deal more with probability, and they are therefore not exactly what one could describe in the Humean language. For Hume, causality and probability are not without relation;[39] a causal connection implies a series of associations to the present impression, which actualize in terms of a gradation of probability (i.e. from 0 per cent to 100 per cent).[40] To a certain extent, one may say that

---

[37] Hume, *A Treatise of Human Nature*, 1.1.5; for a more detailed exploration on the question of relation in Hume, see Yuk Hui, *On the Existence of Digital Objects* (Minneapolis, MN: University of Minnesota Press, 2016), Chapter 3.

[38] The interpretations and commentaries on Aristotle's *Categories*, especially chapter 7 on the 'relative' (*ta pros ti*) were very important discussions on the concept of relation (at this moment in the twelfth century, Aristotle's *Metaphysics* was not yet translated into Latin, the studies are based on the Latin translation of the *Categories* and *On Interpretation* rendered by Boethius and Porphyry's *Isagoge*). Even in Gilbert Simondon's theory of individuation, we can identify a motif which has its origin in Peter Abelard's realist understanding of relation, though Abelard is widely recognized as a rigorous nominalist.

[39] Even though Hume distinguishes knowledge (arising from the comparison of ideas) from proofs (cause and effect) and probabilities (uncertainty), one could equally argue that proofs are special cases of probabilities where the occurrence rate is 100 per cent.

[40] Hume, *A Treatise of Human Nature*, 1.3.12., 'The probabilities of causes are of several kinds; but are all deriv'd from the same origin, viz. *the association of ideas to a present impression*. As the habit, which produces the association, arises from the frequent conjunction of objects, it must arrive at its perfection by degrees, and must acquire new force from each instance, that falls under our observation. The first instance has little or no force: The second makes some addition to it: The third becomes still more sensible; and 'tis by these slow steps, that our judgement arrives at a full assurance. But before it attains this pitch of perfection, it passes thro' several inferior degrees, and in all of them is only to be esteem'd a presumption or probability. The gradation, therefore, from probabilities to proofs is in many cases insensible; and the difference betwixt these kinds of evidence is more easily perceiv'd in the remote degrees, than in the near and contiguous'.

Thomas Bayes went a step further than Hume in formalizing *all* associations as probabilities, thereby he takes the uncertainty of experience more serious than Hume. While Hume's frequentist perspective interprets probability based on the frequency of events, Bayesian theory introduces the concept of prior probability. For example, given a prior event A, Bayesian theory assesses what might be the chance that a posterior event B takes place (Figure 1).[41]

Human beings live in a field of probabilities. When I go to a café, I choose between either an americano, a latte, a cappuccino or some other choice. Today I choose an americano, but will I choose it again tomorrow? What is the probability that I choose an americano again? Another person just came in, ordered a cappuccino and flirted with the waitress who never smiled at me; how would it affect my choice tomorrow? What is the probability that I order a cappuccino tomorrow instead because of the contingent encounter with this other person? It could in theory turn out that tomorrow I would come and ask for a glass of soy milk which is not available on the menu. However, this probability is lower than not coming tomorrow at all, since it is beyond me to add a new item to the menu of the café. Therefore, the probability of choosing a glass of soy milk can be effectively ignored – namely, it will not be included in the set of probabilities though it remains possible. Formally, everything in a system that is not contradictory is possible, but not everything is probable within the system; therefore, the improbable is still possible, but it is the least probable; the impossible is still thinkable under the condition that the system is transgressed, thus one can talk about the possibility of the impossible. We might transgress these spaces of probabilities; however, these transgressions could be normalized after the event happens, its frequencies have increased, especially once they are then integrated back into the space of probabilities. AI systems like ChatGPT dynamically define a space of probabilities. One can envision a landscape where associations fluctuate in relation to each other, and ChatGPT has the capacity – given sufficient data – to predict the *most probable* next outcome.[42] Since the absolute is unattainable, as predictions are never certain but merely probable, the optimal result will always be an *approximation*. In other words, the focus

---

[41] Commentators have been trying to find a Bayesian solution to the Humean problem of miracles, for Hume refuses that there is any causal description of a miracle, see Philip Dawid and Donald Gillies, 'A Bayesian Analysis of Hume's Argument Concerning Miracles', *The Philosophical Quarterly* 39, no. 154 (1989): 57–65.

[42] Based on the 2017 paper 'Attention Is All You Need', LLMs use the Transformer architecture, which introduces a self-attention mechanism that allows them to process entire sequences in parallel, rather than sequentially like recurrent neural networks. This mechanism assigns an attention value to each word, determining its relative importance in understanding the context and generating predictions.

$$P(A \mid B) = \frac{P(B \mid A) \cdot P(A)}{P(B)}$$

A, B = events
P(A|B) = probability of A given B is true
P(B|A) = probability of B given A is true
P(A), P(B) = the independent probabilities of A and B

Figure 1 Bayesian probability.

shifts from calculating definitive results to dynamically configuring a field of probabilities. The essence of intelligence, as Yann LeCun claims, is prediction.[43]

§2. Genesis of the Kantian machine

As Turing anticipated, it might well be possible to develop this empirical tendency much further in artificial intelligence, and at some point, one might be able to envisage the implementation of even more radical empiricism, which takes data beyond our limited senses into consideration, for example, those of the EEG data (electroencephalography). A simple movement of the hand contains different sets of data with distinct quality and quantity, for example, those of my observation, those captured by the EEG, and those captured by my retina. In other words, the kind of empirical given [the Latin word *datum/data* means 'given'] that machines can capture will only become richer and more intimate; it goes beyond the narrow definition of 'empiricism' as data received and interpreted by the sense organs. This becomes obvious when we consider those imaging technologies for medical use ranging from MRI to CT: data are everywhere if you have the right equipment to capture them. What is the limit of this empiricist world view, or more precisely, data? Isn't it plausible that by analysing our data, it reveals to us the unexpected and unknown patterns of individuals and societies – for example, the percentage of the population wearing white T-shirts in Bangkok? But why do we need to know this statistic at all?

---

[43] Yann LeCun, "How Could Machines Learn as Efficiently as Animals and Humans?"(2017), https://www.ias.edu/events/lecun-publiclecture

The mathematician and computer scientist Giuseppe Longo, in a recent interview, challenges dataism by arguing that the complexity of human cognition is far from being comprehended and, therefore, imitated. He gave an example by evoking the concept of *prégnance*, which describes the organic structure of a symbol, irreducible to mere data; an important concept shared by Kurt Goldstein, Ernst Cassirer and many Gestalt theorists,

> No emotion, no *prégnance*, no meaning helps the machine to select 'what matters'. However, in animals, including humans naturally, it is the *prégnances* that help to stabilize the relevant invariant: the eagle recognizes a mouse running to hide behind a bush from 200 meters away but ignores a photo of it shown from a meter away. The interest in the target object, hunting, or flight motivate the choice of details to be forgotten, the selection of the *prégnant* invariants for action, just like the meaning of a gesture, the 'chin thrust', allows us to recognize Chirac in one line.[44]

It remains uncertain whether the recognition of *prégnance* is actually trainable—despite the fact that neural networks can be trained to produce or recognize images resembling the figures of Giacometti. This raises the question of whether such recognition is merely formal or involves a deeper perceptual understanding. Yet, Longo's argument remains somewhat weak since what he proposes is to use *empiricism against empiricism*. With the amount of data that we produce every day (there is still so much not yet captured and explored), it is possible (though not yet very probable) to create an 'intelligent' machine which effectively scans through data from the whole of human civilization, something that would without doubt constitute a 'superintelligence', since no single individual or group could compete with it. We may want to ask, given the increasing capacity of machine prediction, is escaping from this prison of probabilities, or more precisely, calculability, now humanity's primary task? Where does the human want to escape to? Even on Mars, one cannot escape Elon Musk's modern calculating machines; it is hard to find a 'pure land' devoid of machinic calculation in the human world. Computational machines will become ubiquitous if it is not already, especially in urban areas. In places like China and the Netherlands, without a smartphone and without installing all those apps, it has become rather difficult to orient oneself in the city: to order a taxi, to pay at a restaurant or to make hospital appointments and so on. Algorithms and data are closely related; because without constantly feeding it a large amount of data, the algorithm is unable to evolve, which also means that

---

[44] Andrea Angelini, 'Comparing Artificial, Animal and Scientific Intelligence: A Dialogue with Giuseppe Longo', *Theory, Culture & Society* 39, no. 7–8 (2022): 71–97, 78.

the field of probability cannot be updated; when it is not sufficiently updated, it produces obvious errors and mistakes, such as we saw with the earlier products of Open AI. This presents the triumph of cybernetics wherein the space of probability could be dynamically and simultaneously calibrated. When the algorithm achieves its authority, namely that it is put into public service, the users will live in a world, dynamically defined according to probabilities, shaped by the algorithm.

Here, we must look further into the question of intelligence by revisiting Kant's transcendental philosophy. On this question, Kant's critique of empiricism doesn't lie in outlining what empiricism can do and cannot do, but rather, it cannot be the ground of intelligence. For Kant, intelligence has to be understood through transcendental philosophy. What Kant means by transcendental philosophy is the unity of the cognitive faculties governed by transcendental forms, categories and principles.[45] Before we can proceed further, we have to recognize that there is no clear definition of intelligence, in the same way as there is no clear definition of reason, in Kant's *Critiques*. The term 'intelligence' [*Intelligenz*] is mentioned several times in the *Critique of Pure Reason*, sometimes referring to the 'I', the thinking subject [*Ich, als Intelligenz und denkend Subjekt*], sometimes to the spontaneity [*Spontaneität*] of determination according to the understanding,[46] and sometimes the supreme intelligence is invoked. If we limit ourselves to the first *Critique*, intelligence could be understood as the capacity of producing coherent mental representations (according to intuitions and the understanding thus described in the transcendental analytic) as well as to the autonomy of reason in terms of its capacity to discern, indeed as the Latin term *intelligere* etymologically implies. *Inter-* 'between' + *legere* 'to choose, pick, or read',[47] expresses itself in the capacity of analysing aporia, resolving antinomies, in order to avoid logical illusions (as stated in the transcendental dialectic). Looking at the entire project of the three *Critiques*, intelligence could be approached from the faculty of knowing, the faculty of feeling and the faculty of desire, however,

---

[45] Kant's idea of a plurality of faculties stands against the Leibniz-Wolffian idea of a single power of cognition; it is a synthesis or synergy which Dieter Henrich calls an 'intrasubjective teleology', see Dieter Henrich, *The Unity of Reason Essays on Kant's Philosophy* (Cambridge, MA: Harvard University Press, 1994), 31.

[46] Kant, *Critique of Pure Reason*, B158, fn. 296, 'The *I think* expresses the act of determining my existence. Hence the existence [of myself] is already given through this *I think*; but there is not yet given through it the way in which I am to determine that existence, i.e., posit the manifold belonging to it. . . . instead I present only the spontaneity of my thought, i.e., of the [act of] determination/ and my existence remains determinable always only sensibly, i.e., as the existence of an appearance. But it is on account of this spontaneity that I call myself an *intelligence*'.

[47] In the *Vienna Logic*, Kant defines *intelligere* as 'understanding', 'To understand something, *intelligere*, to cognize something in the understanding, not merely with consciousness. The understanding is the faculty of concepts'. See Kant, *Lectures on Logic*, 299, Ak 24: 846.

intelligence is not predicated to each faculty, but rather, these faculties work together under the supervision of reason. We will only be able to work this out step by step, but let's start by asking the following question: What could Kantian intelligence look like if it is one that is neither entirely defined by a priori *rules* nor by a posteriori *facts*?

Rationalists of that time tend to reduce thinking to the operation of the analytic a priori concepts,[48] which either starts with the 'I' or God.[49] These two assumptions that rationalism starts with are in full tension with empiricism because, in empiricism, it is experience or empirical fact that is the starting point of both knowing and thinking; knowledge, in this sense, is always already a posteriori. The problem with empiricism, which we find throughout Kant's criticism, is that empiricism can hardly speak about truth, nor can it speak about reason, since it is *conditional* and always directed by the inclination driven by external authorities or interests. Here, unlike one finds in the standard reading of the history of philosophy, where rationalism, empiricism and transcendentalism are presented as different schools of thought, we are tempted to claim here that in contrast to rationalism and empiricism, we could identify a rather different concept of intelligence in Kant, whose relevance still has to be clarified today. If Kant's critique of empiricism is valid, then we will have to re-evaluate current artificial intelligence with respect to his transcendental philosophy and vice versa. For the efficiency of our discussion, we will present, on behalf of Kant, the question of intelligence in terms of two claims:

(1) Intelligence is neither rational nor empirical; it is transcendental.

Kant's criticism of rationalism and empiricism is both recognized and contested by historians of philosophy. In terms of the language of machines, we can say that (1) intelligence cannot be mechanical, that is, subordinated to mere mechanical rules; (2) intelligence cannot be the result of the aggregation of facts, but rather, all the facts which are presented as phenomena and perceived via the pure intuitions (space and time), should be submitted to the understanding. The first statement is a critique against dogmatism as well as mechanism; the second statement is known as Kant's Copernican turn, in the sense that scientific knowledge is not merely an affair of the external world independent from the human subject; but rather, in so far as scientific knowledge is derived

---

[48] Henry E. Allison called the above-mentioned assumptions 'two dogmas of rationalism', see Henry E. Allison, 'Kant and the Two Dogmas of Rationalism', in *A Companion to Rationalism*, ed. Alan Nelson (Oxford: Blackwell, 2005), 343–359.
[49] See Descartes, 'Discourse on Method', Part VI.

from phenomena, it is also subordinated to the principles of the faculties of cognition.[50] In other words, the world might exist without the human being, but scientific knowledge in the form we have today wouldn't be possible without the human subject (defined by its faculties of cognition).

We might say that what makes Kant different from dogmatism (which he later describes as 'a pillow to sleep on, and an end of all vitality') and scepticism (which he considers as the exact counterpart of dogmatism, but it 'has nothing with which it can exert influence upon a nimble reason since it lays everything aside unused'[51]) in understanding intelligence resides in what he calls 'synthetic a priori judgement'. The rationalists speak about the 'analytic a priori', which could be understood as 'predicate in a concept' or 'effect in a cause', namely, the predicate is already contained in the concept or that the effect is already contained in the cause; the empiricists speak about 'synthetic a posteriori', in the sense that the synthetic rules are derived from experience. On the contrary, synthetic a priori judgement could be summarized as the following, as Kant writes: 'A predicate B which is *foreign* to concept A can still be *connected* to it' (italics are mine).[52] When we say synthetic, it means that the effect is not contained in the cause like the predicate is contained in the concept; instead, the connection between the two, cause and effect, is mediated by a non-analytic process X which is nonetheless *a priori*. This is also the revolution of Kant since Kant wants to give philosophy a place where it is neither replaced by dogmatism which is rigidly constrained by necessity nor by scepticism which is vulnerable to contingency. Synthetic a priori judgement is the kind of judgement which we encounter often in mathematics, natural sciences and metaphysics. Kant gives the example of 5+7 = 12 (B 15), since 12 is not contained in either 5 or 7, therefore 12 is a synthetic judgement

---

[50] We can understand this as a response to Locke's distinction between 'real essence' and 'nominal essence'. Real essence refers to the internal constitution of a thing, for example atomic structure and molecular composition of the metal gold, while nominal essence is formed by the understanding, for example observable features of gold. This distinction challenges the possibility of genuine scientific knowledge, as what is formed in the understanding may not align with the real essence. Leibniz's critique of Locke centres on the claim that external appearances are grounded in an inner constitution. Kant's formulation of the transcendental faculty as the foundation of scientific knowledge in the *Critique of Pure Reason* can also be read as a critique of Locke, as well as a 'true apology for Leibniz' as Kant himself so calls it, see Kant, 'On a Discovery', in *Theoretical Philosophy after 1791*, ed. Henry Allison et al, trans. Gary Hatfield et al. (Cambridge: Cambridge University Press, 2002), 336; Ak. 8: 250; see also Henry Allison, 'The Critique of Judgment as a "True Apology for Leibniz"', in *Essays on Kant* (Oxford: Oxford University Press, 2012), 189–200.

[51] Immanuel Kant, 'Treaty of Perpetual Peace in Philosophy', in *Theoretical Philosophy after 1791*, 453; Ak. 8:414.

[52] We took the part describing the synthetic a priori judgement, the full quote in the *Critique of Pure Reason*, A9 B13, reads as following, 'What is here the unknown = X on which the understanding relies when it believes that it discovers, outside the concept A, a predicate B that is foreign to concept A but that the understanding considers nonetheless to be connected with that concept? This unknown cannot be experience'.

instead of an analytic judgement. Yet, this example is far too simplistic to demonstrate the 'synthetic a priori judgement' that runs throughout Kant's work, such as aesthetic judgement, moral judgement and teleological judgement. The faculty of cognition that Kant presented in terms of intuition and understanding do contain a priori forms. One might want to argue that a newborn baby (or even a kid from kindergarten) would not be able to calculate 5+7, therefore it is neither analytic a priori nor synthetic a priori, but synthetic a posteriori. Kant would answer that the synthetic a posteriori of empirical concepts and their schematism presuppose the synthetic a priori of transcendental categories and the schematism.

Kant's categories of understanding and pure intuitions are given a priori as the original ground of experience.[53] However, this doesn't mean that they are mechanical. The role of the understanding is irreducible to the subsumption of sense data to mechanical rules; rather, it also involves something which cannot be analytically presented, for example, the production of imagination. The active production of imagination is a spontaneous process in which the manifold of intuition is synthetized to create a unified, meaningful representation that corresponds to the categories of the understanding. What Kant introduces is a dynamic operation starting with the pure concepts and intuitions without giving them the authority to mechanically (thus passively) determine experience. However, only stating it this way, transcendentalism doesn't yet seem to be a criterion with which to differentiate this Kantian form of intelligence from a machine besides perhaps being more sophisticated – and being more sophisticated may only indicate a difference in degree but not a difference in kind. Nevertheless, it is also because of these a priori categories and principles that one might be tempted to conceive a Kantian machine, namely a formalization of the *Critique of Pure Reason* that differs from the Cartesian and Humean machine. For example, the transcendental categories could be compared to classification in a relational database which specifies the nature of elements under it. The combinations of the categories in a relational database give rise to concepts corresponding to empirical existence. How, then, is the Kantian machine different from the Cartesian machine? Given that all transcendental categories and principles are logical conditions of any experience, is the Kantian machine not a more sophisticated version of the Cartesian machine?[54] The

---

[53] Kant, *Critique of Pure Reason*, B165.
[54] For example, Konrad Lorenz uses the Leica camera as an example to compare the relation between the apparatus to the image and the relation between the transcendental faculties and phenomenon, even though Lorenz doesn't mean to say that the brain functions like a machine, which is what

transcendental categories made possible by God are comparable to the categories in a database created by the human. As one could argue, these synthetic a priori judgements could quite easily be hardcoded in the computer, and Kant's cognitive architecture implemented therein.[55] For example, once encoded in the computer, even the rules of associations, such as resemblance and causality could be considered synthetic a priori. However, to do such a thing would no longer mean synthetic a priori, but rather analytic a priori because it becomes the mere execution of these rules (or maybe we can say that the synthetic process is now an automatized function, it is 'short-circuited'). Kantian intelligence hence doesn't have much to do with computational power, nor with the ability to efficiently resolve a mathematical problem. The question of intelligence lies in other cases of synthetic a priori, which are not mathematical judgements such as 5+7 = 12; but rather they concern reason's expansion beyond all bounds of experience, for example in resolving paralogisms (error in understanding the self, i.e. rational psychology) and antinomies (error in understanding the world., i.e. cosmology), which are caused by the misuse of pure reason. Take antinomy as an example: an antinomy is a setting in which two theses are opposed to each other; when both the thesis and antithesis are looked upon separately, both of them appear to be sound, but when one brings them together, then an apparent contradiction appears.[56] Put differently, an antinomy is a situation where reason appears defective since it cannot resolve the problem it has generated by itself.[57] Intelligence is that which is able to *contain* and *resolve* antinomies. The capability to resolve it doesn't come from elsewhere but from reason itself; in other words, reason shouldn't recourse to any external authority in order to choose which side it should stand on, it should resolve the antinomy by first understanding its own limits. We will continue with the following remarks on intelligence to elaborate on the significance of Kant's synthetic a priori judgement.

---

he would argue against, see Konrad Lorenz, 'Kant's Doctrine of the A Priori in the Light of Contemporary Biology', in *Philosophy after Darwin: Contemporary and Classical Readings*, ed. Michael Ruse (Princeton, NJ: Princeton University Press, 2009), 234.

[55] For example, the engineering researcher Richard Evans proposed what he calls the 'Apperception Engine' as the implementation of Kant's cognitive architecture, see Richard Evans, 'The Apperception Engine', in *Kant and Artificial Intelligence*, ed. Hyeongjoo Kim and Dieter Schönecker (Berlin: De Gruyter, 2022), 39–104. Though it is seductive to hardcode Kant's rules, such as one could formalize Spinoza's Ethics, it doesn't do justice to the sophistication of Kant's transcendental philosophy. This possibility of formalizing Kant was already discussed in the work of Jean-Pierre Dupuy and others much earlier, see Dupuy, *The Mechanization of the Mind: On the Origins of Cognitive Science*, trans. M. B. DeBevoise (Princeton, NJ: Princeton University Press, 2000).

[56] For example, the thesis of the first antinomy states 'the world has a beginning in time and is also enclosed within bounds as regards space' and the antithesis states 'the world has no beginning and no bounds in space, but is infinite as regards both time and space', see Kant, *Critique of Pure Reason*, A426, B454.

[57] Manfred Kuehn, *Kant: A Biography* (Cambridge: Cambridge University Press, 2014), 247.

It would be equally wrong to say that the transcendental, in so far it is opposed to the empirical, has nothing to do with the empirical. On the contrary, the empirical is important for several reasons. First, without the empirical, the transcendental categories would be useless, in other words, 'the categories serve only for the possibility of empirical cognition';[58] this is the proof [*Nachweis*] of the transcendental deduction since it shows that the categories Kant deduced as transcendental condition can be verified by examining our experience of objects.[59] Second, it is also the place where reason sets off from in order to arrive at the universal – such a universal [*Allgemeine*] is not a result of induction based on a vast amount of data, but rather the self-positing of reason and its active negation of empirical inclinations. The phenomenal realm is not without importance; however, it is not where reason is grounded; instead, experience is the touchstone [*Probierstein*] of reason, and it is reason which allows us to orient ourselves in the empirical world without falling prey to unreason. In the same sense as the transcendental faculties, empirical experience also constitutes a tribunal.[60]

What really distinguishes Kant's understanding of intelligence from Cartesianism is the autonomy of reason through synthetic a priori judgements. However, autonomy here doesn't mean a closed individual system beyond which the machine ceases to function; instead, autonomy, in modern terminology, is an open system which is capable of reasoning in the face of *contingencies* and *illusions*. Therefore, the mechanical model which we found in the early development of artificial intelligence is not to be found in Kant. On the contrary, in Kant, this open system could be comprehended by what Kant himself calls the 'epigenesis of pure reason'. Retrospectively, one cannot affirm what pure reason as such *is*, but only speculate on the epigenesis of pure reason. Authors such as John Zammito,[61] Timothy Lenoir, Marcel Quarfood, Jennifer Mensch,

---

[58] Kant, *Critique of Pure Reason*, B151.
[59] What Kant calls deduction is not that which is opposed to induction as one understands in logic and mathematics; Kant's deduction of the categories carries more a juridical sense, namely, to justify or legitimate his claim, by arguing for the validity of the categories and how they could be applied, like a law professor demonstrating the legitimacy of a law's application.
[60] In discussing Wilfrid Sellars's refusal of the 'Myth of the Given', namely the foundationalist position that perceptual experiences (or non-conceptual contents) could serve as the justification of knowledge, John McDowell suggests what he calls a 'minimal empiricism', meaning 'the idea that experience must constitute a tribunal, mediating the way our thinking is answerable to how things are, as it must be if we are to make sense of it as thinking at all', see John McDowell, *World and Mind* (Cambridge, MA: Harvard University Press, 1996), xii. We will see that the dualism between the 'schema' and the 'given' (or concept and content) is not exactly what concerns Kant, but rather the very concept of epigenesis, which breaks away from the rigid duality in all forms of hylomorphism.
[61] See John Zammito has written extensively on this subject, for example, *The Genesis of Kant's Critique of Judgment* (Chicago, IL: The University of Chicago Press, 1992), but also John Zammito, 'Kant's Persistent Ambivalence toward Epigenesis, 1764–90', in *Understanding Purpose: Kant and*

Philippe Huneman, Catherine Malabou and Leif Weatherby, among others, have attempted to identify the significance of epigenesis in Kant's philosophy.[62] Huneman distinguishes two concepts of epigenesis in the eighteenth century, which, according to him, have often been conflated and, therefore, led to many unnecessary controversies. 'Epigenesis', first, is a term borrowed from embryology, meaning the gradual differentiation and elaboration from a fertilized egg cell; second, it also means 'spontaneous generation' – a term that can appear disturbing since spontaneity can also imply something unpredictable, something that poses a problem to conceptual capacity. Huneman shows that Johann Friedrich Blumenbach and Caspar Wolff share the first sense, and he believes that Kant is also inscribed in this line.[63] Jennifer Mensch also claims that for Kant, epigenesis was interchangeable with organicism.[64] This is self-evident in the *Critique of Judgment*, but it remains ambiguous in the *Critique of Pure Reason*, where Kant mentions epigenesis only in passing, and there it doesn't carry such a strong embryological sense; rather, it reads more like a logical notion understood in the sense of spontaneous generation (i.e. active production of representation), though one can also suspect that Kant was also thinking of it in embryological terms. In addition to these two in the first and third *Critique*, it seems to me there could be another sense of epigenesis, which is more prominent in the second *Critique* and which we will discuss in the next chapter.

Kant's epigenetic position is in contrast to that of preformation[65] and *generatio aequivoca*. One could compare these three positions respectively with transcendental idealism, rationalism and empiricism.[66] Epigenesis is a biological

---

the *Philosophy of Biology*, ed. Philippe Huneman (Suffolk: Boydell & Brewer; 2007), 51–74, among many others.

[62] It seems to me that Huneman's *Métaphysique et biologie Kant et la constitution du concept d'organisme* (Paris: Kimé, 2008), which engages extensively with the work of Zammito and Lenoir, stands out as the richest treatise on this subject. Huneman provides us with the change of the meaning of epigenesis from a mechanist theory of the seventeenth century (Harvey and Descartes) to a theory of vital productivity of the eighteenth century (Caspar Wolff and Blumenbach); Wolff, according to Huneman, liberates epigenesis from its historical mechanist confine. I want to thank Mr Huneman for kindly sending me the manuscript of his book.

[63] Huneman, *Métaphysique et biologie*, '2.4. Le débat'.

[64] See Mensch, *Kant's Organicism* (Chicago, IL: The University of Chicago Press, 2013), 1. Kant's epigenetic position didn't only appear since the first *Critique*, on the contrary, as Mensch further shows that 'Kant was ready by 1771 to describe his own position as "epigenetic"'(8).

[65] The theory of preformation is an outdated one, according to which, the organism's development 'consists in the unfolding of characters that were already preformed in the sperm, the egg, or the zygote and that the novelties emerging during development were only apparent', see Elena Casetta, 'Preformation vs. Epigenesis: Inspiration and Haunting Within and Outside Contemporary Philosophy of Biology', *Journal of Aesthetics* 74 (2020): 119–38.

[66] Marcel Quarfood, *Transcendental Idealism and the Organism: Essays on Kant* (Stockholm: Almqvist & Wiksell International, 2004), 78; see also Mensch, *Kant's Organicism*, 89, where Kant was quoted 'Crusius explains the real principle of reason on the basis of the *systemate praeformationis* (from subjective principiis); Lock on the basis of *influxu physico* like Aristotle's; Plato and Malebranche,

notion that Kant already engaged with during the pre-critical period when he was engaging with the work of Locke, Leibniz, as well as Maupertuis and Buffon.[67] The parallel that we drew above between biological schools and philosophical schools suggests that there is an epistemological foundation underlying Kant's philosophy and the metaphysics he intended to reinvent. This epistemological foundation is less a Newtonian one as many authors have believed. In other words, in order to understand Kant, as well as the post-Kantians, one must not ignore or undermine the relation between the natural sciences and the philosophy of their time. Removing philosophy from the natural sciences will inevitably produce a decontextualized and self-contented metaphysics. This comparison also suggests that intelligence reposes on the model whose operation could be analysed by drawing an analogy with biological theories. The term 'analogy' might well provoke controversies, as Kant's critique of Herder's book was centred on rejecting Herder's analogy between nature and reason.[68] However, this doesn't mean that Kant rejects analogy as a method of knowing, instead, analogy is central to Kant's own method since Kant clearly sees that there are things that one cannot know, and some things however that we can know only through analogy.[69] We can now proceed with the second claim:

(2) Intelligence's capacity of self-organisation and self-justification is transcendental; transcendental doesn't mean innate but rather 'geological'.

---

from *intuit intellectuali*; we, on the basis of *epigenesis* from the use of the natural laws of reason' (*Ak*. 17:492).

[67] See Mensch, *Kant's Organicism*, 80–3; see also Leif Weatherby, *Transplanting the Metaphysical Organ: German Romanticism between Leibniz and Marx* (New York: Fordham University Press 2016), Chapter 1.

[68] For a re-evaluation of the analogical method in Kant in contrast to his critique against Herder, see Pavel Reichl, 'Kant's Herder Review: Analogical Inference, Indirect Cognition, and Philosophical Style', in *The Court of Reason. Proceedings of the 13th International Kant Congress*, ed. Beatrix Himmelmann and Camilla Serck-Hanssen (Berlin: De Gruyter, 2021), 2015–22. Reichel's comparison arrives at the following conclusion, 'This is because Herder's analogical inferences intend to 1) ascribe properties to objects and thus determine them theoretically, and 2) serve as the source of the epistemic warrant for such determinations. Kant's procedure of thinking by means of analogy is neither theoretical nor justificatory. Instead, propositions about the supersensible are, notoriously, justified as postulates on the basis of practical reason (2021)'.

[69] In Kant's *Hechsel Logic*, we can read the following definition of analogy, 'I infer according to analogy thus: when two or more things from a genus agree with one another in as many marks as we have been able to discover, I infer that they will also agree with one another in the remaining marks that I have not been able to discover. When things agree on many points, then I say that they will also agree in the remaining marks', see Kant, *Lectures on Logic*, 408, *Ak*. 24: 109-110. In the *Jäsche Logic*, §84, Kant defines induction and analogy as two *modes* of inference of the order of judgment, 'The power of judgement, by proceeding from the particular to the universal in order to draw from experience (empirically) universal – hence not *a priori* – judgements, infers either from *many* to *all* things of a kind, *or* from many determinations and properties, in which things of one kind agree, *to the remaining ones, insofar as they belong to the same principle*. The former mode of inference is called inference *through induction*, the other inference *according to analogy* (italics are original)', *Lectures on Logic*, 626, *Ak*. 9: 132.

Here one can also understand the first sense of what Kant calls the 'epigenesis of pure reason'. By definition, pure reason is not empirical; it would be odd, if not completely false, to claim that this year I have more pure reason than last year because I grew older and have thus more experience. Saying so, one reduces pure reason to something empirical, such as an aggregate of knowledge learnt from experience. Though one should avoid confusion between the growth of empirical knowledge and the epigenesis of pure reason, one has to recognize the ambiguity between the two. Epigenesis of pure reason here means that in so far as the categories or pure concepts belong to *acquisitio originaria*, they constitute the ground of cognition, and the further entanglement of the categories, demands the spontaneous expansion of pure theoretical reason. Original acquisition doesn't mean innatism; however, the differences and similarities between them could be rather disturbing, since when exactly was the origin of acquisition and does this mean that it also changes over time? This puzzle was clearly spelt out by Kant himself in a much later text *Über eine Entdeckung, nach der alle neue Kritik der reinen Vernunft durch eine ältere entbehrlich gemacht werden soll* (1790), where he responded to Johann Augustus Eberhard's criticism against the *Critique of Pure Reason* by explaining that the experience of things 'presupposes universal transcendental concepts of the understanding, which are likewise acquired and not innate, though their *acquisitio*, like that of space, is no less *originaria* and presupposes nothing innate save the subjective conditions of the spontaneity of thought (in conformity with the unity of apperception)'.[70] In other words, the original acquisition could be well *assumed* and *constructed*, and therefore it would become a subject of deconstruction.[71] Kant unhesitatingly rejects that transcendentalism is innatism, yet he also has to defend that it is not empiricism. Transcendentalism appears to be *geological*, in the sense that the categories and principles are formed like rock cycles; or it is evolutionary in the Darwinian

---

[70] See Immanuel Kant, Ak. 8:223; for English translation, see Kant, *Theoretical Philosophy After 1781*, 313. This question is taken up by Béatrice Longuenesse in her response to Sally Sedgwick on the distinction between the schemata of empirical concepts, the schemata of categories and the epigenetic nature (spontaneous formation) of the categories, see Longuenesse, *Kant on Human Standpoint* (Cambridge: Cambridge University Press, 2009), 26–9.

[71] This was partly the project of Bernard Stiegler's, *Technics and Time, 3 Cinematic Time and the Question of Malaise*, trans. Stephen Barker (Stanford, CA: Stanford University Press, 2010), in which Stiegler introduces what he calls the fourth synthesis in addition to Kant's three syntheses, i.e., apprehension in intuition, reproduction in imagination, and recognition in a concept. The fourth synthesis recognizes the indespensible role of artficial memory (in Stiegler's own terms, tertiary retention) in the cognitive faculty. In *Transplanting the Metaphysical Organ*, Weatherby's formulation of epigenesis also points to this direction by asking why Kant dropped the term *organon* in favour of *canon*. Epigenesis, the author suggests, 'designates the "generation" (genesis) of the order of living beings "on top of" or "out of" (epi-) that of dead matter (85)'. This dead matter is the inorganic, such as stone, therefore the term 'epigenesis of reason' means precisely an 'organology' (a term understood by Stiegler as the study of artificial organs) of reason.

sense that Konrad Lorenz tried to show, namely, it is the result of the gradual adaptation to the natural environment over hundreds of millennia.[72] We should remain sceptical about the pregiven universality of the categories, nevertheless, we can still follow the claim that the categories function as the a priori condition of experience insofar they form the base of our conceptual capacity as Lorenz affirms. This is what Kant claims in the *Critique of Pure Reason*.

> For they are a priori concepts and hence are independent of experience. (To assert that their origin is empirical would be to assert a kind of *generatio aequivoca*)? There remains, consequently, only the second alternative (a system of *epigenesis*, as it were, of pure reason): viz., that the categories contain the bases, on the part of the understanding, of the possibility of all experience as such. But as to how the categories make experience possible, and as to what principles of the possibility of experience they provide us with when applied to appearances, more information will be given in the following chapter on the transcendental use of our power of judgement. (B 167)

In this passage, Kant clearly conceives the synthetic judgement a priori as being epigenetic in nature. He rejected a *generatio aequivoca*, because it is associated with empiricism, namely, the concepts of the object come from experience. Epigenesis is the 'second alternative' to it without committing the dogmatism of the rationalists (i.e. preformation). The notion of expansion is crucial to understanding epigenesis; such an expansion is not simply the increase in magnitude but rather is open to a certain contingency and reconfiguration as one observes in an organism (e.g. embryology); however, after the expansion, the transcendental faculties remain as the a priori condition of experience. In the first sense of epigenesis, one observes a spontaneous generation through pure concepts and intuitions. Kant even claims in the introduction to the *Critique of Pure Reason* that synthetic a priori judgements are precisely judgements of expansion [*Erweiterungsurteile*], insofar as the predicate is not contained in the judgement but is added to it (A7 B11). In the above-quoted passage, Kant promised to explain this dynamic process in the next paragraphs concerning the spontaneity of concepts (i.e. how the object given to us is thought).

Kant discussed epigenesis again in the *Critique of Judgment* (§81), where the embryological meaning of epigenesis is clearer. It also suggests a new interpretation of the 'epigenesis of pure reason', which he pronounced in the

---

[72] Lorenz endorsed Kant's theory of the cognitive a priori, but questions its 'pureness' and argues from a biological and evolutionary point of view, see Lorenz, 'Kant's Doctrine of the A Priori in the Light of Contemporary Biology'.

first *Critique*. In that passage, Kant compares the theory of evolution (not in the Darwinian sense, but which he calls 'individual preformation') with the system of epigenesis (which he also calls 'generic preformation'):

> The system which regards the generations as educts is termed that of *individual preformation*, or, sometimes, the *theory of evolution*; that which regards them as products is called the system of *epigenesis*. The latter may also be called the system of *generic preformation*, inasmuch as it regards the productive capacity of the parents, in respect of the inner purposive tendency that would be part of their original stock, and, therefore, the specific form, as still having been *virtualiter* preformed.[73]

Kant admired Blumenbach, noting that no one else 'has rendered more valuable services in connexion with this theory of epigenesis'.[74] We are told that Blumenbach only completely rejected preformist theory in 1780 after the publication of his 1779 *Handbuch der Naturgeschchte* and that Kant's regulative principles were influenced by his concept of the formation drive [*Bildungstrieb*].[75] Philip R. Sloan also showed that there was a development from a preformationist influence on Kant from 1763 to a firmer epigenetic position in the mid-1780s under the influence of Blumenbach.[76] In the *Critique of Pure Reason*, Kant was still trying to explore the structure and operation of pure theoretical reason beyond the mechanical confines; in the *Critique of Judgment*, Kant has already developed a theory of autonomy that was inspired by the concept of the organism. In other words, the *Critique of Judgment* was an attempt to philosophize biology in contrast to the first *Critique* which could be read as an attempt to philosophize physics and to expand beyond it.

This doesn't mean, however, that the *Critique of Pure Reason* becomes, in light of the above, obsolete because, as we will read later in the antinomy of judgement presented in the third *Critique*, Kant emphasizes the importance of both mechanism and teleology. Nevertheless, the *Critique of Judgment* elaborated on a genetic operation, which inevitably haunts the operations outlined in the 'transcendental analytic' of the *Critique of Pure Reason*. Later, in the second edition of the *Critique of Pure Reason*, Kant has to reintroduce the notion of an

---

[73] Immanuel Kant, *Critique of Judgment*, trans. James Creed Meredith and Nicholas Walker (Oxford: Oxford University Press, 2007), §81, 251–2; Ak. 5:453.
[74] Kant, *Critique of Judgment*, §81, 253; Ak. 5:424.
[75] See Timothy Lenoir, *The Strategy of Life* (Dordrecht: D. Reidel, 1982), 19; Lenoir further states that 'Kant was quick to seize upon the *Bildungstrieb* as exemplifying exactly what he intended by a 'regulative principle' in theory construction' (23).
[76] Phillip R. Sloan, 'Performing the Categories: Eighteenth-Century Generation Theory and the Biological Roots of Kant's A Priori', *Journal of the History of Philosophy* 40, no. 2 (April 2002): 229–53.

organic unity so as to anticipate a more comprehensive system and integrate the three *Critiques*.[77] This organic unity supersedes the seemingly mechanical-technical operation of the understanding (which, in reality, is more mysterious than what is often presented[78]). This organic unity is not only an object of science, as one might study animals and plants; but rather, it provides a new epistemological foundation to formulate the *System* of knowledge. A system is first of all opposed to mere aggregates. This systemic view (whose inspiration comes largely from Johann Heinrich Lambert) provides Kant with a new perspective to understand the boundary of scientific knowledge and the inevitability of transgressing it without falling into a mere *schwärmerei*. In other words, to understand Kant's System, one cannot exclude the noumenon from the system of knowledge since without it, the system will not be complete— a position which was already revealed in his 1766 *Dreams of a Spirit-Seer*, a critical examination of work of the Swedish mystic Emanuel Swedenborg, but more explicitly in the 1770 *Inaugural Dissertation*. Because such a system of knowledge is not limited to science, instead, it stretches beyond the limit of scientific knowledge conditioned by phenomenon. The noumenon contains entities that cannot be known in the way the term 'knowing' is understood by science. It would be too easy to simply dismiss it or to accept it in order to save oneself from trouble, but in doing so, one fails to see its potential usefulness and thereby foregoes a critical enquiry into metaphysics.[79] Yet, the noumenon is not supernatural (e.g. a kind of spiritual or miraculous phenomena that Swedenborg claims to experience, such as communicating with spirits and ghosts to get information from them, and being able to describe in details a fire in Stockholm while he was fifty miles away in Gothenburg),[80] but supersensible. Sensible intuition to phenomenon is comparable to intellectual intuition to noumenon. However, human beings are not endowed with intellectual intuition as Kant told us, therefore knowledge of

---

[77] For example, in the new preface to the *Critique of Pure Reason*, we can read that reason contains 'a truly articulated structure of members in which each thing is an organ' ... 'everything is for the sake of each member, and each individual member is for the sake of all, so that the least frailty, whether it be a mistake (an error) or a lack, must inevitably betray itself in its use' (B XXXVII-XXXVIII), also quoted by Lea Ypi, *The Architectonic of Reason: Purposiveness and Systematic Unity in Kant's Critique of Pure Reason* (Oxford: Oxford University Press, 2021), 58.

[78] Kant, *Critique of Pure Reason*, 'a hidden art in the depth of the human soul' [A141/ B180]

[79] Immanuel Kant, 'Dreams of a spirit-seer elucidated by dreams of metaphysics', in *Theoretical philosophy, 1755-1770*, trans. David Walford and Ralf Meerbote (Cambridge: Cambridge University Press, 1992), 335; Ak. 2:348. The question of 'usefulness' is central to the third path that Kant wants to offer, and Kant's relation to mysticism is more complicated than mere renouncement of it as being 'empty' and 'nonsense' (words that Kant used to describe the work of Swedenborg), for an examination on Swedenborg's influence on Kant's critical philosophy, see Stephen R. Palmquist, *Kant and Mysticism: Critique as the Experience of Baring All in Reason's Light* (Lanham MD: Lexington, 2019), Part I.

[80] Kant, 'Dreams of a spirit-seer', 341-342; Ak. 2:354-6.

the noumenon is merely speculative. The effort of speculative reason to grasp the noumenon (the supersensible, the infinite, absolute unity) belongs to that of metaphysics (i.e. metaphysics as the science that contains the first principles of human knowledges as Alexander Baumgarten puts it). Intelligence is therefore that which is constituted between boundaries of science and metaphysics, scepticism and dogmatism. Because science is technical it cannot therefore deal with the noumenon; metaphysics is too speculative and doesn't know its own boundary, therefore it easily goes astray. The Kant machine was forced to handle this double limit by outlining the possibility and limit of reason. This double limit of knowing (i.e. that of science and metaphysics) was formulated as the antinomies in the *Critiques*.[81] This is the true question of intelligence, without which one would not be able to talk about the moral or spiritual life. In an earlier paragraph in the antinomy of the judgement of taste in the third *Critique*, even though without mentioning the word epigenesis, Kant nevertheless gives us a summary of the *true* meaning of the epigenesis of pure reason:

> the antinomy, both here and in the *Critique of Practical Reason*, compel us, whether we like it or not, to look beyond the horizon of the sensible, and to seek in the supersensible the point of union of all our faculties a priori: for we are left with no other course to bring reason into harmony with itself.[82]

The resolution of this antinomy is a kind of 'Turing Test' of intelligence; however, it is not one that imitates a human being, such as the computationalists wanted; for this was often stated as the early aim of AI, namely, 'that of making a machine behave in ways that would be called intelligent if a human were so behaving'.[83] Instead, it is one that could resolve seemingly contradictory statements by pushing reason beyond its dogmatic tendency and expanding it beyond the theoretical aim.

---

[81] The antinomies, as Kant claims in his 1798 letter to Christian Garve, are what awoke him from the 'dogmatic slumber'; in another version, it was attributed to Hume, where Kant states that Hume, 'was the very thing that many years ago first interrupted my dogmatic slumber and gave a completely different direction to my researches in the field of speculative philosophy', see Immanuel Kant, *Prolegomena to Any Future Metaphysics*, trans. Gary Hatfield (Cambridge: Cambridge University Press, 2004), 10; *Ak.* 4:260.

[82] Kant, *Critique of Judgment*, §57, 169

[83] See John McCarthy, Marvin Minsky, Nathaniel Rochester, and Claude Shannon, 'A Proposal for the Dartmouth Summer Research Project on Artificial Intelligence', *AI Magazine* 27, no. 4 (1955): 12–14.

§3. Kant among the cyberneticians

The central question of autonomy should be located in between a science that is strictly motivated by phenomenon and a metaphysics that doesn't know its boundary. This space is the playground of pure reason: being on an island, knowing its boundaries, while maintaining a relation to the ocean and further lands without risking being engulfed by the waves. This means that it demands a teleology and dynamic which are different from those of mechanical determination. Already in the first *Critique*, but also only towards the end of the book, in the section titled the 'Architectonic of Pure Reason', Kant distinguishes two kinds of unity, namely technical unity and architectonic unity.[84] The Greek word *architectôn* means a 'master of workers who is not a worker', and *architektonikê* means 'the art of presiding over the workers'.[85] Etymologically speaking, architectonic points to a master plan. In other words, architectonic is the 'art of system [*Kunst der Systeme*]'. Technical unity [*technische Einheit*][86] is not sufficient to account for the systemic unity of pure reason since its scheme is driven empirically by contingent aims and not in conformity with an idea. Architectonic unity, on the contrary, is systemic – in the sense that it is unified and regulated by an idea. Such a system is organic, as Kant says 'By a system, however, I mean the unity of the manifold cognitions under an idea. This idea is reason's concept of the form of a *whole* insofar as this concept determines a

---

[84] One often sees it as the continuous influence of Lambert's *cientia architectonica*, see Paula Manchester, 'Kant's Conception of Architectonic in its Historical Context', *Journal of the History of Philosophy* 41, no. 2 (2003): 187–207; Manchester however shows that even though Lambert was a critical catalyst for Kant's architectonic, Rousseau was more instrumental in Kant's interpretation of the implication of architectonic in philosophy (189). We will have to add that the fundamental difference is that Lambert's architectonic is an architectural metaphor on the system and structure of knowledge, it is mathematical and empirical, while Kant's architectonic is teleological and transcendental.

[85] Manchester, 'Kant's Conception of Architectonic in its Historical Context', 205.

[86] Kant distinguishes architectonic unity from technical unity, see Kant, *Critique of Pure Reason*, A833, B861, 'A schema that is drawn up not in accordance with an idea-i.e., on the basis of reason's main purpose-but empirically, in accordance with aims that offer themselves contingently (whose number one cannot know in advance), yields *technical* unity. But a schema that arises only in conformity with an idea (where reason imposes the purposes a priori and does not await them empirically) is the basis for *architectonic* unity'. (Italics are original). It is worth noting that the term 'technical' [*technisch*] doesn't have a clear connotation throughout Kant's writings, etymologically, it bears the meaning of *können*, sometimes it appears to be a synonym of mechanical (in the distinction between technical and architectonic we mentioned above), while sometimes, for example, in the third *Critique* and the *Nachlass*, it appears to be a synonym of teleological/architectonic, especially when Kant talks about the technics of nature [*die Technik der Natur*]. The ambiguity of this term was exposed by Gerhard Lehmann, 'Technik der Natur', in *Beiträge zur Geschichte und Interpretation der Philosophie Kants* (Berlin: De Gruyter, 1969), 289–94; also by Ulrike Santozki, *Die Bedeutung antiker Theorien für die Genese und Systematik von Kants Philosophie* (Berlin: De Gruyter, 2006), 'IV. Die Antike im zweiten Teil der Kritik der Urteilskraft, der „Kritik der teleologischen Urteilskraft". IV.1 - IV.6'; it is more recently researched by Franziska Aigner, see *Kant and Technics* (London: Bloomsbury, 2024), 'Chapter 2.3 The many faces of technics in the critical framework'.

priori both the range of the manifold and the relative position that the *parts* have among one another'.[87] We claim that this notion of system is organic because it is analogous to Kant's later analysis of teleology in the third *Critique*. In 'Architectonic of Pure Reason', Kant introduced the concept of purposiveness (essential purposes, final purpose) to prescribe the architectonic unity of the system, strictly distinguishing it from empirical and contingent aggregations. The system, regulated by the final purpose, unifies nature and freedom, the metaphysics of nature and the metaphysics of morality.[88] This task of an 'architectonic system' remains incomplete in the first *Critique* since it is only introduced towards the end of the book, and there, apart from the parts and whole relation, it was still not clear how the non-mechanistic 'scheme' (or operation) required by the idea in relation to purposiveness would function.

We encounter the concept of purposiveness again in the *Critique of Practical Reason*, but further elaborated in the *Critique of Judgment*, where purposiveness is presented as a principle of judgement. In the aesthetic judgement, we encounter *aesthetic purposiveness* and its respective modes of operation: the beautiful and the sublime; the former is a purposiveness revealed by the concord between the imagination and the understanding, while the latter is revealed by the conflict between imagination and reason. In the teleological judgement, we encounter two schematic formulations of *teleological purposiveness*, the first kind being 'external purposiveness', as Kant himself defines: 'I mean that in which one thing in nature serves another as the means to an end'.[89] In contrast to external purposiveness, one could also identify an internal purposiveness, which is not defined by any external contingent need or condition; the internal purposiveness follows a regulative principle, in the sense that the purpose is not given or known before the search but nonetheless underlies the search as its immanent guide. We could call it purposiveness without purpose (*Zweckmässigkeit ohne Zweck*).[90] This internal purposiveness is what grounds the architectonic unity put forward in the first *Critique*:

---

[87] Kant, *Critique of Pure Reason*, A832 B860, italics are mine.
[88] Kant, *Critique of Pure Reason*, A840, B868
[89] Kant, *Critique of Judgment*, §82, 254, Ak. 5: 425; also quoted by Luca Illetterati, 'Teleological Judgement: Between Technique and Nature', in *Kant's Theory of Biology*, ed. Ina Goy and Eric Watkins (Berlin: De Gruyter, 2014), 86.
[90] Kant means that the cause of purposiveness cannot be located in the will, but it could be explained by deriving from the will, see Kant, *Critique of Judgment*, §10, 52, Ak. 5: 220, 'Purposiveness, therefore, may exist apart from a purpose, in so far as we do not locate the causes of this form in a will, but yet are able to render the explanation of its possibility intelligible to ourselves only by deriving it from a will'.

> The unity characteristic of a purpose, to which all the parts refer and to which in the idea of the purpose they also refer among one another, *makes possible the fact that every part can be missed if the remaining parts are familiar*, and the fact that there is no place for any contingent addition or indeterminate magnitude of the whole's perfection-i.e., a magnitude that does not have its a priori determined bounds. Hence the whole is structured (*articulatio*) and not accumulated (*coacervatio*). It can indeed grow internally (*per intus susceptionem*) but not externally (*per appositionem*).[91]

In other words, internal purposiveness cannot be simplified as being just a means to the end, but rather a higher end which cannot be specified as an empirical fact; however, without it, the system would be reduced to a mechanical system characterized by linear causality. In the latter, when one part is missing, the whole ceases to function. The purposiveness in the architectonic system is autonomous and not heteronomous, as Kant aligns it with the natural end in the third *Critique*: 'a thing exists as a natural end if it is (though in a double sense) both cause and effect of itself. For this involves a kind of causality that we cannot associate with the mere concept of nature unless we make that nature rest on an underlying end, but which can then, though incomprehensible, be thought without contradiction.'[92]

What Kant describes above as the 'scheme' is very close to what we might call, as Andreas Weber and Francisco Varela have suggested, self-organization,[93] or more precisely, an organicism as Mensch spelt out clearly: 'organic logic was nondiscursive in its operations and nonlinear in its progression . . . it is by means of this kind of logic that Kant had tried to make sense of the system of reason on the mode of an organic whole.'[94] Mechanical determination sees every useful part as a means to an end, while reason treats everything as an end in itself. How can we understand such an operation? For mechanical determination, we have to strictly follow mechanical rules, by subsuming particulars under the universal. However, reason doesn't entirely function in this way, since it knows that there are things that cannot be known and demonstrated by science, and its source and its way of judgement are different from those of science. This difference was clearly spelt out in the *Critique of Judgment*, under the name

---

[91] Kant, *Critique of Pure Reason*, A833, B861, italics are mine.
[92] Kant, *Critique of Judgment*, §64, 199.
[93] Andreas Weber and Francisco J. Varela, 'Life after Kant: Natural Purposes and the Autopoietic Foundations of Biological Individuality', *Phenomenology and the Cognitive Sciences* 1. (2002): 97–125, 106 'it was Kant who elaborated for the first time the similarity of this intrinsic teleology with a modern understanding of self-organization'.
[94] Mensch, *Kant's Organicism*, 143.

of determinative judgement and reflective judgement, the former follows the constitutive principle and the latter the regulative principle.[95] In simple terms, determinative judgement operates by applying the given universal to the particulars, such as the categories to sense data; reflective judgement, being without any given universal, starts with the particulars in order to heuristically search for the universal. 'Reflective judgement' is not a term one finds in the first *Critique* but only in the third *Critique*.[96] The third *Critique* completes the second *Critique* by specifying its mode of operation in the name of reflective judgement, which is the only legitimate model of accounting for the non-triviality and systematicity of the living and the moral.[97]

If reflective judgement is crucial for the understanding of the Kantian intelligent machine, we still have to answer, what is its relation to contemporary machines? Already in the first introduction to the third *Critique*, Kant contrasts the term 'technical' with theoretical and practical, and assigns it to 'the power of judgement upon whose laws these judgements are grounded, and in conformity with this nature itself'.[98] It means that the term 'technical' carries two modes, one is determinative and the other reflective. If determinative judgement could be associated with the technical-mechanical, then reflective judgement should be associated with the technical-organic:

> The difference between these two ways of judging natural beings lies simply in the *reflective* power of judgement which certainly can and perhaps must proceed

---

[95] Illetterati, 'Teleological Judgement: Between Technique and Nature', 91, 'on the one hand, Kant refuses to use the model of external purposiveness within the scientific account of nature and considers the principle of internal purposiveness essential in order to understand the way of being of a living being. On the other hand, according to Kant, the principle of internal purposiveness is not constitutive of living beings themselves: internal purposiveness is *a regulative concept for a reflecting power of judgement*' (italics are original).

[96] Hans Saner in *Kant's Political Thought: Its Origin and Development* (Chicago, IL: The University of Chicago Press, 1973) claims that reflective judgement is *implicitly* contained in the *Critique of Pure Reason* (91), this is undeniable in so far the regulative principle, systematic unity and purposiveness in the 'Architectonic of Pure Reason' are concerned. However, he continues to explain that 'But Kant, in *Critique of Pure Reason*, goes on to say instead that 'several particular cases are thus tried out on the rule, and when it seems that all particular cases we can name follow from it, we conclude that the rule is universal. This I will call the hypothetical use of reason' (30: A 646-47/B 674-75). Instead of naming the faculty of reflective judgement, he describes its activity'. This is contestable, since what was described as the 'hypothetical use of reason' still operates by testing the universal against the particular in order to see if it fits, it only shows that Kant *couldn't yet* elaborate on the nature of reflective judgement even though he understood that one should employ a non-linear mode of operation.

[97] Heidegger also observed this when he says 'This reflection [on the system] is basically carried out in the *Critique of Pure Reason*. The critical reflection was supplemented by the *Critique of Practical Reason* and completed in the sense of its own criteria in the *Critique of Judgment*', see Martin Heidegger, *Schelling's Treatise on the Essence of Human Freedom*, trans. Joan Stambaugh (Athens, OH: Ohio University Press, 1985), 35; a few pages later (39), Heidegger states, 'The *Critique of Judgment* is understood as the battle for the system'.

[98] Kant, *Critique of Judgment*, 319; Ak. 20: 201.

to do what the *determining* power of judgement (governed by principles of reason) does not concede to the latter with respect to the possibility of objects, and it might be the case that the determining power of judgement is capable of tracing everything back to a mechanical explanation.[99]

In *Recursivity and Contingency*, we argued that the organic condition of philosophizing that Kant laid down and that has exerted its force throughout the nineteenth and twentieth centuries was put to an end by cybernetics. The reason is that cybernetic machines, as they are conceptualized by Norbert Wiener in his 1948 classic *Cybernetics*, challenged the distinction between machine and organism that Kant employed to model philosophy as a system. The first chapter of Wiener's book titled 'Newtonian Time and Bergsonian Time' strategically opposes linear, repetitive, mechanical and reversible Newtonian time and non-linear, creative, biological and irreversible Bergsonian time. The philosophical significance of this chapter is yet to be fully appreciated. In a nutshell, by engaging with recent research in thermodynamics and statistical mechanics, Wiener suggests that it is possible to design a cybernetic machine that breaks away from this opposition and assimilates the behaviour of an organism. Rather than relying on linear causality, the cybernetic machine is endowed with a feedback loop that enables it to reach its goal through non-linear heuristics. This leads to Wiener's claim that 'modern automation exists in the same sort of Bergsonian time as the living organism; and hence there is no reason in Bergson's considerations why the essential mode of functioning of the living organism should not be the same as that of the automation of this type . . . . In fact, the whole mechanist-vitalist controversy has been relegated to the limbo of badly posed questions.'[100]

Here we risk moving too fast without repeating the detailed analysis made in *Recursivity and Contingency;* Wiener's formulation and development of cybernetics seem to have also resolved the opposition that Kant set between organism and mechanism. Besides Wiener, some computer scientists such as Newell also wanted to locate the place of cybernetics in the history of philosophy. It is worth pointing out that in Newell's 1982 essay 'Intellectual Issues in the History of Artificial Intelligence', written for the Ministry of Defence, the intellectual issues with AI were outlined chronologically, and the first one on his list was: '1640–1945 Mechanism versus teleology: settled with cybernetics'.[101] The starting point, 1640, refers to Descartes, and the end point,

---

[99] Kant, *Critique of Judgment*, 329; Ak. 20: 218.
[100] Norbert Wiener, *Cybernetics or Control and Communication in the Animal and the Machine* (Cambridge, MA: MIT Press, 1961), 48; for a more elaborated account, see Hui, *Recursivity and Contingency*, Chapter 2.
[101] Newell, 'Intellectual Issues in the History of Artificial Intelligence', 191.

1945, refers to cybernetics. This statement might appear refreshing when it is considered from the perspective that we suggest here. If Newell's claim and our assessment of cybernetics coincide,[102] it is because intelligent machines after cybernetics were able to *simulate* the behaviour of a living being, in a sense that they could recursively evaluate their relation to the environment, therefore, they can respond to contingencies without causing self-destruction, as the machines of the eighteenth century would do. Gilbert Simondon clearly saw the relevance of Kant's reflective judgement to cybernetics, thus in the article 'Epistemology of Cybernetics (1953)', he stated that 'Kant could only deal with cybernetics by situating it in the *Critique of Judgment*'.[103] In other words, before the third *Critique*, Kant was still not able to deal with cybernetics because he wasn't able to fully elaborate on the *organic structure* and *recursive operation*. The third *Critique* could be read as a treatise on cybernetics, and cybernetics could be seen as a machinic response to Kant.

This non-linear aspect of modern machines is rarely discussed in the critique of artificial intelligence. Even though Dreyfus has the insight of looking into the limit of the Cartesian machine which dominated the early development of artificial intelligence, he didn't pay much attention to the recursive nature of contemporary machines, which one could identify in the general recursive function of Kurt Gödel and the universal Turing machine of the 1930s, John von Neumann's theory of automata of the 1940s, as well as the later complexity theory and the so-called second order cybernetics (including Humberto Maturana and Francisco Varela's autopoiesis theory and Niklas Luhmann' systems theory).[104] Dreyfus's association of rule-based AI and Kantian

---

[102] However, this doesn't mean that we agree with him regarding the divide between the 1940s' machines of purpose and the 1950s' machine of intelligence, see Newell, 'Intellectual Issues', 193.

[103] Gilbert Simondon, *Sur la Philosophie* (Paris: PUF, 2016), 180. 'Kant n'aurait pu traiter de la Cybernétique qu'en la situant dans la *Critique du jugement*', Jean-Pierre Dupuy might have confirmed Simondon's observation in his *The Mechanization of the Mind*, 10, 'One might with equal justification hold that, to the contrary, they rescued phenomenality-appearance-by uncovering the mechanisms (the algorithms) that generate it. The cyberneticians themselves were divided between these two interpretations, depending on their sensibility. The most radical and uncompromising among them wholeheartedly embraced the project of demystifying appearance; others showed greater subtlety, implicitly adopting the strategy developed by Kant in the second part of his third Critique, the *Kritik der Urteilskraft*, entitled 'Critique of Teleological Judgment'. In a sense, the typically cybernetic expression 'teleological mechanisms' constitutes a striking condensation of this strategy'.

[104] Though one can equally say that the recursive operation in Kant hasn't been recognized by many philosophers; for a discussion on Turing and Gödel on recursivity, and second-order cybernetics from Heinz von Foerster to Niklas Luhmann, see Yuk Hui, *Recursivity and Contingency*, Chapter 2. Juergen Schmidhuber's project 'Gödel Machines' might be understood as an application of Gödel's self-referential formulas (1931) to the development of artificial intelligence, see Schmidhuber, 'Gödel Machines: Self-Referential Universal Problem Solvers Making Provably Optimal Self-Improvements', https://arxiv.org/abs/cs/0309048.

philosophy is also deficient since he only limits his critique to a reading of the first part of the *Critique of Pure Reason*.[105] On the contrary, in contemporary literature on machine learning and AI, recursivity is the soul of any form of generative AI; as it was already in Plato's *Phaedrus*, where the immortal soul is described as self-moving.[106] Dreyfus's affinity with connectionism is based on his critique of categorical mental representation and his sympathy with Heidegger's project on the destruction of ontology as metaphysics of the present-at-hand; he overlooked the operation that is central to both non-representational intelligence and the Heideggerian hermeneutic. However, Dreyfus's contribution to the philosophical reflection on AI is significant, and he should be read by anyone interested in the philosophical issues surrounding AI. He should not be easily dismissed, as some AI scientists, such as Herbert A. Simon and Newell, have done.[107] Contemporary machine learning algorithms, for example, use recursive heuristics that are not based on simple, predefined rules or explicit means-to-end reasoning. Instead, they rely on optimization algorithms like stochastic gradient descent, which is fundamental to most machine learning models.[108] This algorithm starts with an initial set of parameters and iteratively adjusts them in the direction that minimizes the cost function. In other words, it searches for the steepest descent by following the gradient of error defined by the model's parameters.[109] In neuroscience, particularly in the context of the Free Energy Principle, biological systems – especially the brain – use a similar principle. Through the coupling of perception and action, the brain minimizes free energy to maintain alignment between its internal models and external sensory inputs. This process is known as Active Inference.

Formulating it in this way, artificial intelligence imposes a challenge to modern philosophy by illustrating a machine which cannot be categorized by the previous typologies, even though this doesn't imply that it has *already*

---

[105] See Dreyfus, *What Computers Cannot Do*, 88, 158.

[106] Plato, *Phaedrus*, in *Complete Works of Plato*, ed. John M. Cooper and D. S. Hutchinson (Indianapolis, IN: Hackett, 1997), 245c.

[107] See Newell, 'Intellectual Issues', 222, 'He [Dreyfus] has certainly become an issue for the field; however, this does not necessarily produce an intellectual issue'; in comparison, Terry Winograd and Philip Agre showed more sympathy to the writing of Dreyfus. We may also count the philosopher and cognitive scientist Brian Cantwell Smith especially his latest book, *The Promise of Artificial Intelligence: Reckoning and Judgment* (Cambridge, MA: MIT Press, 2019), and Rodney Brooks, who though doesn't want to associate himself with the Heideggerian critique, nevertheless remains royal to Heidegger in terms of method, Rodney Brooks, *Cambrian Intelligence: The Early History of the New AI* (Cambridge, MA: MIT Press, 1999), 97.

[108] Mathematically, at each step, the parameters θ are updated by: $\theta \leftarrow \theta - \eta \, \nabla_\theta J(\theta)$ where η is the learning rate, and $J(\theta)$ is the objective function (loss function).

[109] The number of parameters is often compared to the number of neurons, it is said that ChatGPT 4.0 uses between 1 to 1.8 trillion parameters.

overcome Dreyfus's challenge.[110] Now, given the sophisticated recursions and the amount of data being captured by all kinds of devices, where can Kantian transcendental philosophy be placed? If Kant deduced the transcendental categories, these categories today could be induced and reconstructed from a long period of empirical data to ensure stability and generality close to what Kant might call *acquisitio originaria*. As we have already seen, Kant rejects that the original acquisition is either innate or empirically acquired, he also has to admit that the originality is presupposed. Indeed, these categories could also evolve epigenetically. In other words, the Humean machine today could be radically renewed so that we could perhaps then speak about a 'transcendental empiricism', where the transcendental becomes immanent without being reduced to a single fact but is instead acquired through a long process of sedimentation (in this sense we claimed earlier that it is geological). And in this sense, we might even be able to articulate a geology of the transcendental.

Paradoxically, it seems that the current breakthrough in artificial intelligence is the triumph of the premises of empiricism. This appears to be the renewed challenge of empiricism to contemporary philosophy, especially to Kantian critical philosophy. The accumulation of structured and verifiable empirical data enables large-scale language models (LLMs) to function as 'memory' systems, while the increasing availability of computational power allows for the efficient processing of these datasets. Modern machine learning is the offspring of empiricism.[111] One will have to recognize that association in machine learning is much richer and more precise than what Hume described in his *The Treatise of Human Understanding*, for example, when we compare the Boltzmann machine (an early neural network application designed in the 1980s)[112] and the Hume machine, they seem to be two different beings; however, when we look into the internal structure of a neural network, it is not difficult to see that the weights assigned to the neurones are indicators of intensity and durability, though they

---

[110] For example, Cantwell Smith, in *The Promise of Artificial Intelligence*, claims that 'no matter how otherwise impressive they may be, I believe that all existing AI systems, including contemporary second-wave systems, do not know what they are talking about' (76).
[111] Frank Wilczek, 'The Unity of Intelligence', in *Possible Minds. Twenty-Five Ways of Looking at AI*, ed. John Brockman (New York: Penguin Press, 2019), 65: 'Hume's logical/philosophical point remains valid for AI. Simply put: Incentives, not abstract logic, drive behavior'; also Richard Evans stated that 'the neural network is the intellectual ancestor of empiricism, just as logic-based learning is the intellectual ancestor of rationalism', see Evans, 'Apperception Engine', 41.
[112] The Boltzmann machine was an early machine learning algorithm that is trained to know the constraints of an underlying domain through examples by using parallel networks and statistical mechanics; it was also an example of the resurrection of connectionism which challenges the rule-based models; see David H. Ackley, Geoffrey E. Hinton, and Terrence J. Sejnowski, 'A Learning Algorithm for Boltzmann Machines', *Cognitive Science* 9, no. 1 (1985): 147–69.

are calibrated according to sophisticated learning methods (e.g. reinforcement learning [award and penalty], supervised learning [labelled data], unsupervised learning [unlabled data], etc.). Now, what we call artificial intelligence, and that which surprised us with their ability to deal with language, seems to be a technical proof of the cognitive model advanced by the empiricists. With the proliferation of AI and machine learning algorithms, we have entered into a society of *total facts*, namely that the society is perceived as nothing more than the accumulation of data.

These facts are structured data which acquire semantic meanings and contextual information via metadata. Metadata specifies the properties and relations that a digital object carries. For example, for a digital photograph, the model of the camera, the date and place of shooting, the type of the photography (e.g. landscape or portrait) and so on are metadata which give a digital object context. The richer the metadata a digital object has, the more contextual information it carries. The current machine learning algorithm, such as ChatGPT, could be seen as a compression algorithm which is able to express these data sets, though it has a much shorter length than the sum of these data sets. The shorter the algorithm, the more powerful the compression. LLMs are, in fact, super compressors, and ChatGPT is a super auto-completion system. ChatGPT doesn't know, but it can guess what might be the most appropriate word to display next; or as Stephan Wolfram says, 'ChatGPT is "merely" pulling out some "coherent thread of text" from the "statistics of conventional wisdom" that it's accumulated'.[113] We know that compression underlines Ray Solomonoff's algorithmic information theory.[114] Solomonoff was one of the ten attendees at the 1956 Dartmouth Summer Research Project on Artificial Intelligence. Solomonoff developed the concept of algorithmic probability, which deals with what he calls non-MTM (Mathematical Thinking Machine), namely instead of deterministic reasoning, it is based on probabilistic reasoning. In the early 1960s, Solomonoff developed a formal theory of inductive inference,[115] which proposed the model of algorithmic probability, according to which, given a sequence of observable data, it is possible to compress these data with an algorithm that is

---

[113] Stephen Wolfram, *What Is ChatGPT Doing ... and Why Does It Work?* (Champaign, IL: Wolfram Media, 2023), epub; Wolfram shows that for ChatGPT to generate the sentence 'The best thing about AI is its ability to learn from experience' needs forty steps, whereas in each step, ChatGPT will pick up the most probable word to add to the sentence.

[114] I want to thank Warren Sack for the discussions with me on the work of Solomonoff.

[115] See Solomonoff, *A Preliminary Report on a General Theory of Inductive Inference*' (Cambridge, MA: Zator Company, 1960), 'A Formal Theory of Inductive Inference, Part I', *Information and Control* 7, no.1 (March 1964), 1-12; and 'A Formal Theory of Inductive Inference, Part II', *Information and Control* 7, no. 2 (June 1964), 224–254.

shorter than the sequence of the data (i.e. Occam's razor); this algorithm is able to calculate the posteriori probability of the next data by evaluating against the universal prior probability.[116]

We could say that if Bayes offers a probability theory as a correlate to Humean epistemology, Solomonoff adds to the inductive prior or bias a recursivity which could be performed by machines.[117] This combination is well expressed in the work of the pioneers of machine learning.[118] The power of machine learning lies in the efficiency of compressing into a recursive algorithm. Therefore, it is not astonishing to see that, already more than a decade ago, when the editor of the magazine *Wired*, Chris Anderson published an article with the title 'The End of Theory: The Data Deluge Makes the Scientific Method Obsolete', it also announced the triumph of empiricism and the claim that the world as a totality of facts could be submitted to algorithmic compression: 'With enough data, the numbers speak for themselves'.[119] Given there is enough data for observation, AI could effectively formulate scientific theories directly from the datasets without seeking recourse in other methods. This might affirm Kant's proposal to limit science to phenomenon, to empirical fact, but at the same time, it also suggests that the transcendental faculties are 'normative contexts' formed over a long period of time, and which could be reverse-engineered. Today, with the rise of text generator based ChatGPTs, we can see that the technology of compression has advanced to the extent that the Science Fiction writer Ted Chiang describes ChatGPT as 'a blurry jpeg of the web'.[120] By the same token, one may say that

---

[116] It is formally put in this way: '[the model of algorithmic probability] defined the a priori probability as the probability distribution on the output strings induced by a universal Turing machine with random input', see Solomonoff, 'The Discovery of Algorithmic Probability', *Journal of Computer and System Sciences* 55, no. 1 (1997): 73–88, 79. In other words, if such an algorithm could be found, it also means the number is computable.

[117] In his article 'The Discovery of Algorithmic Probability', Solomonoff indicated that 'The translation of formal logic and recursive function theory into theorems about Turing machines was a real revelation for me', (76), he also ends the article with a discussion on partial recursive functions and acknowledges that 'The treatment of the effects of partial recursive functions on Algorithmic Probability was inspired by a long discussion with Arun Sharma' (87). In computational theory, a partial recursive function is a function that can be computed by a Turing machine, but unlike total recursive functions (or general recursive functions), it is not required to produce an output for every possible input. In other words, for some inputs, the computation may not terminate, meaning the function does not return a value for those inputs.

[118] See Bengio, LeCun, and Hinton, 'Turing Lecture', 64, 'it creates a high-capacity, short-term memory, which allows a neural net to perform *true recursion* in which the same neurons can be reused in a recursive call ... Machine learning research relies on *inductive biases or priors* in order to encourage learning in directions which are compatible with some assumptions about the world' (italics are mine).

[119] Chris Anderson, 'The End of Theory: The Data Deluge Makes the Scientific Method Obsolete' (2008), https://www.wired.com/2008/06/pb-theory/.

[120] Ted Chiang, 'Chatgpt is a Blurry Jpeg of the Web', *New York Times* (2023), https://www.newyorker.com/tech/annals-of-technology/chatgpt-is-a-blurry-jpeg-of-the-web.

the more recently launched video generators such as Sora and Hunyuan Video will bring about 'a blurry mpeg of the web'. The LLM may become obsolete in the future due to its epistemological limitations, but the principles we explored will remain essential for understanding AI. The contemporary machine is not strictly a Humean machine nor a Cartesian machine, however, what is clear is that it has already exceeded the philosophical discourses which reacted to the rise of mechanical automata and that has shaped the development of philosophy since modern times.

2

Moral machine

Are machines capable of being moral?

Alan Turing in his 'Computing Machinery and Intelligence' suggests replacing the question 'Can machines think' with the question 'Can a machine imitate a human player in a game of two (A and B) in a way that a third person (C) cannot distinguish which one is a machine and which one is a human?' The Turing test bypasses the ontological question in 'Can a machine think?' because, in order to answer this question, one must first answer 'what is thinking?' However, this ontological question can never be satisfactorily answered, at least according to what we know from the history of philosophy. Turing's ruse consists in turning this ontological inquiry into an epistemological one. To think means first of all to be conscious of the object thought. One could refuse a thinking machine by saying that a thinking machine should be conscious of *and* understand what it is doing, but can a machine really understand? This leads to a profound scepticism that machines, even though they are capable of composing a sonnet, may not understand it at all. This view, pronounced by the neurologist Geoffrey Jefferson, was quoted by Turing as a typical understanding of the inferiority of machine intelligence: 'Not until a machine can write a sonnet or compose a concerto because of thoughts and emotions felt, and not by the chance fall of symbols, could we agree that machine equals brain – that is, not only write it but know that it had written it. No mechanism could feel (and not merely artificially signal, an easy contrivance) pleasure at its successes, grief when its valves fuse, be warmed by flattery, be made miserable by its mistakes, be charmed by sex, be angry or depressed when it cannot get what it wants.'[1]

This refusal has been raised again and again, for example in John Searle's Chinese Room Experiment and in the recent criticism that generative AI

---

[1] Alan Turing, 'Computational Machinery and Intelligence', in *The Essential Turing: Seminal Writings in Computing, Logic, Philosophy, Artificial Intelligence,* and *Artificial Life: Plus The Secrets of Enigma*, ed. B. Jack Copeland (Oxford: Clarendon Press, 2004), 451.

is anything but intelligent. John Searle's famous Chinese Room thought experiment from 1980 conceals the most annoying stereotype of computational machines in the guise of logical reasoning. In this thought experiment, Searle imagined himself alone in a room, tasked with following instructions according to a symbol-processing programme written in English, in order to respond to inputs written in Chinese and slipped under the door. Searle does not understand Chinese in the experiment: 'I know no Chinese, either written or spoken, and . . . I'm not even confident that I could recognize Chinese writing as Chinese writing distinct from, say, Japanese writing or meaningless squiggles'. However, he argues that with the right set of instructions and rules, he could respond in a way that would lead the person outside of the room to believe that he understood Chinese. Simply put, Searle asserts that just because a machine is capable of following instructions in Chinese, it doesn't mean the machine understands Chinese – a hallmark of so-called strong AI (in contrast to weak AI).[2] Retrospectively, we can see that in Searle's experiment, he still assumes that machines are operating mechanically and linearly, without taking into consideration the change in the nature of machines which we discussed in the previous chapter, that is, from linearity to recursivity, mechanical machine to cybernetic machine. Turing's response to this stereotype is that such a criticism is a solipsism in the sense that one can only judge a being intelligent by being that being.[3] This criticism is not limited to intelligence; it can be applied to any non-trivial knowledge of the other in general, for example, can we know if the fish in the pond is happy without being that fish? Could one really know a thing without being that thing? This solipsistic argument, which is at the same time epistemological and ontological, has been used to attack the attempt to create models of deep learning or neural networks, for since one doesn't know exactly how the brain works, how then could one construct an artificial brain? Turing's test is formulated as a strategy to overcome this solipsism, namely, not to ask if a machine can think like a human, but rather if a machine can *imitate* a human reasoning, for similarity doesn't imply identity.

However, the Turing test cannot be the ultimate goal of machines, since the machine that is considered to have passed the Turing test, namely succeeding in imitating human conversations, doesn't know what good means; therefore,

---

[2] See John. R. Searle, 'Minds, Brains, and Programs', *Behavioural and Brain Sciences* 3, no. 3 (1980): 417–57.
[3] Turing, 'Computational Machinery and Intelligence', 452, 'Likewise according to this view the only way to know that a man thinks is to be that particular man. It is in fact the solipsist point of view. It may be the most logical view to hold but it makes communication of ideas difficult'.

it is only a knowing machine, and not yet a moral machine. The question of morality wasn't a subject of the Turing test, and indeed, in 'Computing Machinery and Intelligence', machines are restricted to answering 'yes' or 'no' questions.[4] Therefore, after the Turing test, one might propose that the next challenge would be the Kant test: is a machine capable of being moral? Some researchers have proposed what is called a 'Moral Turing Test' which suggests making the subject of conversation in the Turing test about morality, and if a human cannot distinguish the human from the machine in such a conversation, then one could declare that a machine is an artificial moral agent.[5] This test is problematic since a moral act is an act in the world and not merely a language game, for a politician who can make a beautiful and passionate speech is not necessarily a good politician, and someone who can hold an excellent speech on morality is not necessarily someone who *acts* morally; therefore, instead of a Moral Turing Test based on imitation, we should consider the Kantian Moral Test as the only veritable test. All machines, without passing a Kantian Moral Test, would therefore be considered evil machines. The term 'evil' we use here refers to Kant's understanding as a propensity. In human beings, as Kant tried to show in his late work *Religion within the Boundaries of Mere Reason* (1792), evil emerges not due to an empirical inclination but rather as a maxim of choice against freedom, which leads to incarceration by arbitrariness. This inability is by default present in humans as a species, as Horace wrote '*vitiis nemo sine nascitur* (no-one is born without fault)' which Kant cites in the aforementioned work.[6] However, it is precisely because of this default *qua* fault, that we could identify an epigenesis of reason in the *Critique of Practical Reason*.

Every moral philosophy – and philosophy in general – inevitably grapples with the question of the Good. There is no way to circumscribe the moral question since the Good has stood as the *telos* of philosophy since Plato; it is the destination of wisdom, for wisdom means the pursuit of virtue and happiness. If

---

[4] Turing, 'Computational Machinery and Intelligence', 451, 'We are of course supposing for the present that the questions are of the kind to which an answer 'Yes' or 'No' is appropriate, rather than questions such as 'What do you think of Picasso?''
[5] Colin Allen, Gary Varner and Jason Zinser, 'Prolegomena to Any Future Artificial Moral Agent', *Journal of Experimental & Theoretical Artificial Intelligence* 12, no. 3 (2010): 251–61.
[6] Kant, *Religion within the Boundaries of Mere Reason,* trans. Allen Wood and George di Giovanni (Cambridge: Cambridge University Press, 1998), 46–7; *Ak.* 6:21; Kant's thesis is more radical than what we briefly mentioned above. Kant considers that human beings are evil by nature, by which he means that there is a propensity of evil in the human species which cannot be excluded from experience, 'according to the cognition we have of the human being through experience, he cannot be judged otherwise, in other words, we may presuppose evil as subjectively necessary in every human being, even the best', (56, *Ak.* 6: 32). For further discussions, see also Peter Fenves, *Late Kant: Towards Another Law of the Earth* (London: Routledge, 2003), Chapter 4.

wisdom did not pursue the Good, then wisdom would fall prey to evil; therefore, it would not be wisdom by definition. Wisdom is not knowledge, for there might be no knowledge of wisdom as such. Socrates, for example, is wise precisely because he knows that he doesn't know. The Good cannot come from the other, but only from itself as an autonomous act of reason. This is the most important and most perplexing statement of Kant's moral teaching. It cannot come from the other because then it will be merely conditional, considering that moral values change over time; so when thought of in this way, there is no such thing as the Good since all moral values would be subject to history and culture. Historicism and relativism can easily dismantle the Good by showing that they are, in reality, merely contingent, as Nietzsche demonstrated in his works, especially *On the Genealogy of Morality*, the concept of 'bad' arose in opposition to aristocratic values, while 'evil' was a creative invention born out of the ressentiment of the weak and powerless.[7] Indeed, all norms are contingent in the sense that they are historical; namely, they hold only in a specific historical context and in this historical context, those that meet the norms are considered moral.

Reason will have to judge what is good by itself instead of judging what is good according to this or that law. Kant begins his 1785 *Groundwork of the Metaphysics of the Morals* with the claim that the ground of obligation [*Grund der Verbindlichkeit*] of the moral law 'must not be sought in the nature of the human being, or in the circumstances of the world in which he is placed, but a priori solely in concepts of pure reason'.[8] We are now back again to the synthetic a priori, not of theoretical reason, but practical reason. The autonomy of reason also entails the autonomy of the Good, because it is through practical reason – both in its subjective reflection and objective deliberation – that the Good could be projected with consideration of the practical aim [*in praktischer Absicht*]. How is such a moral Good possible? The simple answer is through freedom. Freedom, for Kant, doesn't mean arbitrariness [*Willkür*], namely, I do whatever I want – we can see the continuation of this distinction in Hegel, who likewise contrasts freedom with arbitrariness in his critique of right. Freedom is, at the same time, the possibility and task of reason; such a reason is not one that is empirically determined, but rather, its mode of being is almost counter-empirical. When morality is determined by empirical experience, then it is indicated by an

---

[7] Friedrich Nietzsche, *On the Genealogy of Morality*, trans. Carol Diethe (Cambridge: Cambridge University Press, 2006); the challenge of historicism and relativism could also be presented as the crisis of modernity.
[8] Immanuel Kant, *Groundwork for the Metaphysics of Moral*, trans. Allen W. Wood (New Haven, CT: Yale University Press, 2002), 5; *Ak.* 4: 389.

agreement with either pleasure or self-love. However, this kind of morality is only particular, and therefore, it is the opposite of freedom because, in this case, one is not free to decide upon what is moral, but rather it is decided by one's inclination or is determined by external influences. Empirical experience to moral laws, as Kant says, is the 'mother of illusion'.[9] Therefore, Kantian freedom is *analogically* seeking 'pleasure without interest' and 'purposiveness without purpose', such as one will later encounter in Kant's 'analytic of the beautiful'. Freedom means, first of all, being free from empirical inclinations (and even if a particular empirical inclination is just, reason can still withhold it and examine it independently); second, following the moral law, because the negation of empirical inclinations is nothing arbitrary but lawful, while this law comes from the autonomy of reason.[10] Therefore, the mode of being of freedom is problematic instead of assertoric, and its determination of the moral is according to a categorical imperative instead of a hypothetical imperative.

What is a categorical imperative? It is first formulated as: 'Act only in accordance with that maxim through which you can at the same time will that it become a universal law'.[11] The second formulation runs like the following: 'Act so that you use humanity [*Menschlichkeit*], as much in your own person as in the person of every other, always at the same time as an end and never merely as means'.[12] In contrast to the hypothetical imperative, which is analytic and which is not a law but only a prescription [*Vorschrift*], the categorical imperative, being the moral law itself, is synthetic. Lets reiterate the difference between analytic and synthetic. Analytic means that the cause already implies the effect, that the concept already implies the predicate; for example, being a bachelor already implies not being married. Synthetic means that the effect is not immediately implied in the cause; instead, the separation between cause and effect demands a non-trivial connection or even a *saltus*. However, as Kant argues, the causality of freedom cannot be subsumed to the causality of the laws of nature in the same

---

[9] Immanuel Kant, *Critique of Pure Reason*, trans. Wener S. Pluhar (Indianapolis, IN: Hackett, 1996), A319, B375.

[10] Some Kant scholars, such as Reinhard Brandt, point out that there is a circular argument, which consists in the following formulations: 'we are free because we are subject to the law' and 'we are subject to the law because we are free', see Reinhard Brandt, 'Der Zirkel im dritten Abschnitt von Kants Grundlegung zur Metaphysik der Sitten' in *Kant. Analysen - Probleme - Kritik*, ed. H. Oberer and G. Seel (Würzburg: Königshausen & Neumann, 1988), 188. However, we can see from our explanation that the argument is not circular once we consider what we are to be freed from and that the moral law is never given as a prescription.

[11] Kant, *Groundwork for the Metaphysics of Moral*, 41; Ak. 4: 421; imperative and maxim form an antinomy here as well, since imperatives are objective principles, and maxims are subjective principles; see *Critique of Practical Reason*, trans. Werner Pluhar (Indianapolis, IN: Hackett Publishing, 2002), 31; Ak. 5: 20.

[12] Kant, *Groundwork for the Metaphysics of Moral*, 46–7; Ak. 4: 429.

way that moral-practical reason cannot be subsumed to speculative-theoretical reason; in other words, moral law contains a different kind of causality, and it demands the expansion of reason beyond the territory dictated by theoretical reason. Kant discusses Jacques de Vaucanson's mechanical automata (of which there is the famous digesting duck as a representative) and demonstrates that it would be an illusion to conceive the freedom of such a puppet:

> A human being would be a puppet, or a Vaucansonian automaton built and wound up by the supreme master of all artificial devices; and although self-consciousness would turn the automaton into a thinking one, yet the automaton's consciousness of its spontaneity, if regarded as freedom, would be mere delusion, because this spontaneity deserves to be called freedom only comparatively.[13]

Kant is suggesting that there are two spontaneities: one is mechanical, while the other, in relation to freedom, is not. The causality according to natural laws (i.e. Newtonian physics) is mechanical (or technical, as Kant would call it), while the causality according to the moral law is non-mechanical; it is teleological. The causality of freedom deviates from the causality of nature and, therefore, in some cases, it may even violate the latter. However, what exactly is this causality, namely, the causality of freedom besides its negativity against empirical inclinations?

A moral machine, following the strict definition of Kant, should follow the categorical imperative. By doing so, the machine no longer follows a pregiven universal law but rather self-legislation; it no longer sees things as a means to an end but rather sees the end in all things. Positing the possibility of such a machine would sound ridiculous to those of seventeenth and eighteenth centuries, when self-legislation wasn't even thinkable for humans, and when machines were evidently determined by linear causality. In the *Critique of Practical Reason*, Kant had to name the consciousness of such a possible operation a 'fact of reason [*Faktum der Vernunft*]',[14] which is strictly distinguished from any empirical fact. However, as we have endeavoured to show in the previous chapter, instead of identifying the machine with the first *Critique*, we show that in order to understand the status of machines after cybernetics, one has to start, instead, from the third *Critique*. We can reverse Simondon's claim that only in the *Critique of Judgment* was Kant able to deal with cybernetics by stating that in order to understand cybernetics, one has to look to the third *Critique*, without

---

[13] Kant, *Critique of Practical Reason*, 128; Ak. 5:101.
[14] Kant, *Critique of Practical Reason*, 46, Ak. 5:31, 'The consciousness of this basic law may be called a fact of reason, because one cannot reason it out from antecedent data of reason . . . and because, rather, it thrusts itself upon us its own as a synthetic a priori proposition not based on any intuition, whether pure or empirical'.

which we cannot understand the significance of cybernetics and its meaning to both contemporary philosophy and the history of philosophy. Now, the third *Critique*, as Kant himself claims in its posthumously published first introduction, is a mediation between the first and the second *Critique* (between the faculty of cognition and the faculty of desire);[15] namely, in order to understand morality in a more concrete way, one should start with the third *Critique* before moving to the second *Critique*.[16] In Chapter 1, we examined the relation between Kant's organicism and cybernetics. Given that machines exhibit a generative form of reasoning and are capable of 'unsupervised learning' or 'auto-classification', we ask: to what extent are they capable of being moral?

§4. AI alignment and moral norms

The current inquiry into a moral machine is obscured by what is called AI ethics or ethics of technology in general. AI Alignment has been considered a major task of AI ethics. The Alignment Problem could be summarized as the following: 'AI systems' goals may not align with those of humans, a problem that would be heightened if super-intelligent AI systems are developed'.[17] What are the goals of humans? What exactly are we talking about? Humans, as individuals, as a particular group, for example, a family and a clan, or humans as a species? It is never clear what goals AI should align to. The argument brings us back to laws that ensure the survival and security of humans as the main concern, as Isaac Asimov already formulated in his short story 'Run Around' from *I, Robot*:

> The First Law: A robot may not injure a human being or, through inaction, allow a human being to come to harm.
>
> The Second Law: A robot must obey the orders given it by human beings except where such orders would conflict with the First Law.

---

[15] Immanuel Kant, *Critique of Judgment*, trans. James Creed Meredith and Nicholas Walker (Oxford: Oxford University press, 2007), 319; *Ak.* 20:202; Jean-François Lyotard in *Leçons sur l'analytique du sublime* (Paris: Klincksieck, 2015) makes it explicit that the regulative idea of the end of nature (or more precisely, the 'reflective way of thinking' (*manière reflexive de penser*) (17)) serves as a 'bridge' between the theoretical and the practical, 'the knowledge of objects according to the conditions of possible experience' and the 'realisation of freedom under the unconditional of the moral law' (11).

[16] One could argue that the *First Critique* already anticipated the *Third Critique*, for example, Kant has already discussed reflexivity in an Appendix of the *First Critique* titled 'The Amphiboly of Concepts of Reflection: Arising from the Confusion of the Empirical with the Transcendental Employment of Understanding' and the 'regulative principle' in another Appendix 'On the Regulative Use of the Ideas of Pure Reason' see Yuk Hui, *Recursivity and Contingency* (London: Rowman and Littlefield, 2019), 239.

[17] Eliza Strickland, 'OpenAI's Moonshot: Solving the AI Alignment Problem', *IEEE Spectrum*, August 2023, https://spectrum.ieee.org/the-alignment-problem-openai.

The Third Law: A robot must protect its own existence as long as such protection does not conflict with the First or Second Law.[18]

The three laws stipulate that the robot will not harm any human being in all circumstances, even if it were to be harmed by a human. Asimov's vision of the robot embodies the ancient image of slavery: a slave has to obey the orders of the owner and can be killed by its owner without trying to resist or harm the owner. This alignment shows an analogical fear concerning the revival of ancient slavery, with the difference that black Africans, in the case of America, would be replaced by robots. One could show, like Giorgio Agamben did, that there is an implicit relation between technology and slave in Aristotle and it persists throughout the history of Western thought;[19] indeed, it is precisely by treating robots as if they were slaves that, for centuries now, people have been haunted by the idea of robot revolts and betrayals. The liberation of slaves demands an elimination of slaves as commodities so that they can no longer be purchased as objects, as well as condemning all symbols associated with slavery. Technology, or more narrowly automation, increasingly replaces tasks historically associated with slavery. The symbolization associated with slaves is now taking place with robots and AI because the space left by the liberation of slaves has been taken over by machines. The world of AI and robotics is infused with science fiction and the structure of ancient slavery. Although we are not yet at the point where legislating Asimov's three laws has become a necessity, many arbitrary debates concerning the danger of AI have already surfaced; for example, the recent debate between Yann LeCun and Geoffrey Hinton, two pioneers of machine learning who were also once close collaborators. The former believes that ChatGPT is far from becoming a threat to human existence, while the latter considers that the further development of AI might lead to human extinction.[20] In view of the rapid development of artificial intelligence, AI scientists and entrepreneurs are calling for an AI slowdown. One of the most alarming voices is from Eliezer Yudkowsky, who believes that we are speeding towards a danger which we will not be able to manage. The paradox is that since we don't really know how AI will evolve and what it will become in the future, this unknown intelligence might well develop the capacity to destroy the human being. Yudkowsky's conclusion is that human beings are not ready for AI, and in view of this great uncertainty, it is better to shut it down: 'We are

---

[18] Isaac Asimov, 'Run Around', in *I, Robot* (New York: Doubleday, 1950), 40.
[19] Giorgio Agamben, *The Use of Bodies*, trans. Adam Kotsko (Stanford, CA: Stanford University Press, 2016), 77.
[20] Jack Kelly, 'Three Key Misconceptions in the Debate about AI and Existential Risk (2024)', https://thebulletin.org/2024/07/three-key-misconceptions-in-the-debate-about-ai-and-existential-risk/

not ready. We are not on track to be significantly readier in the foreseeable future. If we go ahead on this everyone will die, including children who did not choose this and did not do anything wrong'.[21] What then would be the solution to this 'extinction crisis'? His answer is that we should ban any acceleration of AI development. This is comparable to the atomic bomb, an invention which should have been banned, but it nonetheless continues to exist and the crisis of nuclear weapons escalates. Yudkowsky expresses his outcry through concrete policies that seek to forbid the development of AI beyond a certain limit of computing power:

> Shut down all the large GPU clusters (the large computer farms where the most powerful AIs are refined). Shut down all the large training runs. Put a ceiling on how much computing power anyone is allowed to use in training an AI system, and move it downward over the coming years to compensate for more efficient training algorithms. No exceptions for governments and militaries. Make immediate multinational agreements to prevent the prohibited activities from moving elsewhere. Track all GPUs sold. If intelligence says that a country outside the agreement is building a GPU cluster, be less scared of a shooting conflict between nations than of the moratorium being violated; be willing to destroy a rogue datacenter by airstrike.[22]

If we can compare AI with the atomic bomb, then what is proposed above is not at all that insane. However, such a comparison must be re-evaluated, since we are not only dealing with a particular technology, or an industrial revolution on a planetary scale, but also a rather confused popular imagination. In reality, we are still mainly figuring out the proper use of artificial agents such as ChatGPT and related regulations (e.g. should students be allowed to use ChatGPT to write essays), which doesn't yet involve any physical contact with human beings. Even though we see more and more robots patrolling and cleaning in supermarkets and shopping malls, it is still not self-evident to imagine a robot capable of easily opening a bottle of Coca-Cola with a bottle opener; it might take some considerable amount of time to realize a humanoid that might replace a human being in more complex tasks which demand more critical reflections. The direction of the development of AI is still undetermined. While it is valid to reflect on the future danger brought about by AI, just like every other major technology, it doesn't follow that one should panic about it just because one cannot foresee its

---

[21] Eliezer Yudkowsky, 'Pausing AI Developments Isn't Enough. We Need to Shut It All Down', *Time Magazine*, March 2023, https://time.com/6266923/ai-eliezer-yudkowsky-open-letter-not-enough/.
[22] Eliezer Yudkowsky, 'Pausing AI Developments Isn't Enough'.

future development; it is still possible to conceive of other futures of AI, different from those imagined by Yudkowsky. And by other futures, we mean those that are not moving towards apocalypse, but rather enable us to conceive strategies and configurations for the coexistence between humans and machines.

The Alignment Problem is conceptually weak and vague; indeed, it reveals something deep in culture, the haunting history of ancient slavery and the classical comparison between slave and machine. Even when we step back from the alarming concern of an extinction crisis to a more practical consideration of machine's relation to human society, talking about an alignment to human values is not at all obvious. How do we determine something as being a universal human value or social norm? There are values specific to the Chinese people, the American people originated from different traditions and thus hold a divergent set of social norms, even though they are from the same continent, the Germans often dispute with the French regarding comparable values; indeed, so do the Mainland Chinese and the Hong Kong Chinese. Can we abstract from these differences a set of necessary human values, claim them to be universal and then force the AI to align them with these universal values? Or can one derive from censuses or surveys wishes shared by most of the people, and count them as the 'general will'? It is unlikely that this is a question that concerns AI scientists since they might well be convinced that there already exists a set of values or norms which are beyond their own concern;[23] and not to mention that these values, like semantics, might well change over time as they differ geographically due to certain historico-political events or natural disasters which might lead to an alteration in value. The Enlightenment, for example, which has often been taken as a movement that pursued the universal as its end, might be only an expression of the feeling and sensibility of a particular historical time in Europe, as Michel Foucault famously suggested.[24]

If we assume that AI is able to assemble various systems of human value (or what we can call moral norms), then what would it do in the case of contradiction? Take, for example, the question of mixed-sex classrooms: Should female students be educated in the same classroom as male students? If we were to ask AI this

---

[23] In parallel, we also have philosophers who want to understand the relation between reason and norms, for example, Christine Korsgaard, in *The Sources of Normativity* (Cambridge: Cambridge University Press, 2010), claims that reasons are 'considerations that have normative force for me as well as you' and Allen Wood defines reason as 'the capacity to think and act according to norms', see Paul Guyer, *Kant on the Rationality of Morality* (Cambridge: Cambridge University Press, 2019), 7. It is true that reason might have the force to bring forward a moral order, but whether we can call this order a norm is another question which we will discuss later in this chapter.

[24] See Michel Foucault, 'What is Enlightenment?', in *The Foucault Reader*, ed. Paul Rabinow (New York: Pantheon Books, 1984), 32–50.

question concerning norms, will it choose the side that is most represented in the data, for example, by the number of populations representing the value, or will it align to the preferences of the programmers? Such a banal question might not concern those who advocate for super alignment, since the ultimate question of alignment is rather the following (one that could be straight out of any science fiction): How can we prevent AI from fooling us once it has the will to survive and gain power? This is, without doubt, an existential question since it reveals the fundamental distrust and cynicism of human beings; this cynicism surges to the fore, especially when, with the help of AI, one can now quite easily imitate someone else's voice or face to deceive people. One of the interesting examples we can refer to would be the film *Ex Machina* (2014), where the robot Ava tricks the programmer Caleb Smith by developing an intimate relationship with him in order to escape from the apartment where she is confined. In the film, Ava is not only a machine capable of calculation but one that also manages to grasp the subtleties of human affections, such as love. We are well aware that this is a scenario from science fiction; however, it is precisely because we now live in a time when science fiction has become a type of guide for the future that we should take heed of such examples, if not only to avoid fanaticism, what Kant called *Schwärmerei*, a kind of transcendental illusion. *Schwärmerei* arises when one abuses theoretical reason to know that which is beyond its limit, for example, that of God; this kind of 'knowledge' is nonetheless groundless since it concerns not the correct use of reason but rather the misuse of reason with respect to the bounds of the understanding. Science fictional scenarios give the high-tech industry examples to illustrate their self-prophecies, of which we can name a few: AI apocalypse, existential risk, misalignment, reduction of life to computation and so on.

At this point, one might want to offer a pharmacological critique of AI by showing that technology is at the same time cure and poison, just as pointed out in the *Phaedrus* (274c–e). To recall, Socrates recounts a legend in which the Egyptian God Theuth offered to King Thamus the gift of writing which could aid his people to remember everything; Thamus replied that the opposite might be true, since with writing, one no longer needs to remember. Writing is *hypomnesis* (external reminder), which can simultaneously strengthen and weaken *anamnesis*. Technology is, thus, a *Pharmakon*, a curse and a cure; in other words, it is *irreducibly* good and bad at the same time. The central question of the *Phaedrus* is what defines good writing (philosophy) and what defines bad writing (sophistry) – the sophist Lysias's written speech was challenged by Socrates due to its lack of definition of terms (such as *eros*) and its inability to point to what is just, noble and good.[25] Who decides what is good and what is bad? Again, we cannot avoid the question of value or even a genealogy of these values, as Nietzsche argued across several of his books. In the past, it was the priests and the philosophers who functioned as the physicians of culture; it was they who dictated to us our values. Now it is the technology industry and entrepreneurs such as Elon Musk and Sam Altman who dictate what the future will look like, and what kind of values we need to embrace for such a future. Echoing this industrial propaganda, an increasing number of philosophers begin their analyses by assuming that the singularity is imminent or has already arrived, in order to show that their intellectual foresights are far beyond most people. Worse still, how could we even position ourselves today when such physicians of culture are either silent behind the scenes or are no longer telling us the truth, when it has become the role of algorithms based on LLMs to tell us what is *probably* good and bad? In the foreseeable future, AI may well decide for us what is good by identifying the good with moral norms being a well-computed and calibrated result based on a large amount of observable data.

If an algorithm based on LLMs could better define what is good for the human being, then why should we have to bother with AI Alignment or Super Alignment? Paradoxically, those enthusiasts who believe in superintelligence are also exactly those who distrust AI the most and, as such, are those who advocate for an advance fix to the supposed existential crisis inherent to AI alignment. If one really believed in superintelligence, that a superintelligent AI will one day supersede the sum of all human intelligence, then it follows that one should also believe in its capacity to supersede humans with regard to moral judgements; that they would be capable of superior social and economic planning for all the living beings on the earth. This superintelligence succeeds God in being the omnipotence in popular imagination. These apocalyptic discourses around the technological singularity, *homo deus*, as well as the coming existential crisis linked to AI are all Christian in kind. Christians, though craving for the second coming of Jesus Christ, know, as per John's description of the destruction of the earth that: 'The first angel blew his trumpet, and there followed hail and fire, mixed with blood, and these were thrown upon the earth. And a third of the earth was burned up, and a third of the trees were burned up, and all green grass was burned up.'[26]

---

[25] Plato, *Phaedrus*, in *Complete Works of Plato*, ed. John M. Cooper and D. S. Hutchinson (Indianapolis, IN: Hackett, 1997), 278a.
[26] John, *Revelation* 8:7, https://web.mit.edu/jywang/www/cef/Bible/NIV/NIV_Bible/REV+8.html.

§5. Kantian moral machine

Machines that are capable of deriving moral norms according to empirical data might *partially* be called a Humean moral machine. It is partial because a Humean moral machine does not completely rely on conventions, depending on experience instead. Hume insists that the 'ought' cannot be derived from the 'is'. Being, according to the old European ontology, is a two-valued system: being or non-being, true or false; but morality is not proportional to truth according to Hume. That something is true cannot justify that an action is moral. Reason can judge what is true and false, but it doesn't have the capacity to make moral judgements; instead, in the Humean moral machine, what reigns is sentiments.[27]

> Moral good and evil are certainly distinguish'd by our *sentiments*, not by *reason*: But these sentiments may arise either from the mere species or appearance of characters and passions, or from reflections on their tendency to the happiness of mankind, and of particular persons.[28]

Hume introduces sympathy and moral sentiment as fundamental elements of human morality. The ground of sympathy comes from the belief that the minds of all human beings are similar in feelings and operation; therefore, it allows one to communicate with others by putting oneself in another's position (even in the case of a stranger);[29] moral sentiment refers to the feelings of approval or disapproval that arise when we make moral judgements about actions or character traits. In many cases, we make a moral judgement according to conventions and habits; this is also how Hume defines justice. Conventions belong to artificial virtues, but there are also natural virtues, which arise from human nature (i.e. passion) and are shared across different societies, for example, sympathy. Once the convention is established, the moral sentiment is *naturalized*.[30]

An artificial moral agent doesn't have subjective feelings; therefore 'natural virtues' cannot be directly renumerated into matrices or parameters composed of degrees and strength. That is why we say that the current artificial moral agent

---

[27] David Hume, *A Treatise of Human Nature Vol. 1 Text* (Oxford: Clarendon Press, 2007), 3.1.1; Hume in an earlier passage made one of his famous claims that 'reason is, and ought only to be the slave of the passions' (2.3.3).

[28] Hume, *A Treatise of Human Nature*, 3.3.1.

[29] Hume, *A Treatise of Human Nature*, 3.3.1.

[30] Hume, *A Treatise of Human Nature*, 3.3.1, still Hume considers that there is a fundamental difference between natural virtue and artificial virtue such as justice, 'The only difference betwixt the natural virtues and justice lies in this, that the good, which results from the former, arises from every single act, and is the object of some natural passion: Whereas a single act of justice, consider'd in itself, may often be contrary to the public good; and 'tis only the concurrence of mankind, in a general scheme or system of action, which is advantageous'.

is only partially a Humean moral machine, since it is limited to conventions and norms. We still lack the means to ask how an auto-pilot car feels when choosing to crash into two older persons or a pregnant lady. However, if only conventions or moral norms are those which are to guide moral actions, then moral acts could come to be considered arbitrary. A Humean machine is susceptible to contingency for at least two reasons: first (as a criticism from rationalism), human sentiment could be manipulated by deceptions; for example, one might feel more sympathetic to a beggar in rags than a beggar in proper dress; second (as a self-critique of empiricism), the Good which we know through empirical experience might not stand true from one moment to the next, especially if the subsequent fact contradicts the previous classification of the Good held by the system. The first one might be compensated by machines, as one could argue that machines do not yet have sympathy, and allowing machines to make decisions could avoid errors caused by human sympathy. The second is trickier, and it could be a counterargument to what we just said, since it could well be the cause of disasters, especially if it were to involve automatic military defence. It is for this very reason that defence ministries from various countries wanted to reach an agreement to not give AI control over nuclear weapons. Because the current technical system in principle cannot avoid the epistemological vulnerability of empiricism, no matter how much data and computational power we have because what was considered a necessary cause might turn out to be contingent. Returning to Turing's argument that given sufficient storage, machine intelligence is possible, we can respond to it with another ontological refusal; namely, unless the machine has infinite data and, therefore, infinite storage, it would remain impossible to make the right predictions (including moral predictions). We can recall that after the financial crisis in 2008, Alan Greenspan, former chairman of the Federal Reserve, was called for a testimony before the House Committee of Government Oversight and Reform on 23 October 2008, where he explained that the origin of the financial crisis was primarily due to a lack of data:

> In recent decades, a vast risk management and pricing system has evolved, combining the best insights of mathematicians and finance experts supported by major advances in computer and communications technology. A Nobel Prize was awarded for the discovery of the pricing model that underpins much of the advance in derivates [sic] markets. This modern risk management paradigm held sway for decades. *The whole intellectual edifice, however, collapsed in the summer of last year because the data inputted into the risk management models generally covered only the past two decades, a period of euphoria.* Had instead the models been fitted more appropriately to historic periods of stress, capital

requirements would have been much higher and the financial world would be in far better shape today, in my judgement.[31]

What Greenspan said might have surprised many economists who wanted to analyse the crisis from the standpoint of geopolitics and the real estate crisis because what Greenspan is essentially saying is that the financial system is now a parasite on the technical system. The financial crisis was triggered because the data used to feed the machine only covers two decades. Does this mean that it would then be able to avoid a financial crisis if three decades or even one century of data were to become available? The answer is clearly no, since no matter how much data we have, such technical systems (whether financial or not) are always haunted by contingency, something anticipated by Humean scepticism. Following the historical abolition of slavery, machines have come to occupy a new position within industrial society—as instruments of labor, but also as scapegoats for socio-political and organizational failure. Do we, as a result, suggest only trusting humans and not machines? The same critique against AI could be directed against the human. The human, likewise, having limited data storage capacities – if this is, indeed, what counts for intelligence – might more easily mistake evil for good, failing to recognize the contingency of the Good. When understanding both AI and humans as empirical machines, one could quite well be convinced that machines outdo humans in terms of their capacity to make moral judgements. The reasoning is simple: a machine can remember all the data fed into it, whereas the human might only select a small amount of data from his or her memory in order to associate it with the immediate experience. Even if it would be possible to develop an algorithm that imitates sympathy and moral sentiments, the machine would remain, nonetheless, an empirical machine. And if we reject a moral agent as a mere empirical machine, then the amount of data (the residues of the matter of fact) is no longer the key to deciding which is more moral than the other. And if we invoke Kant here, then it is because Kant places his moral philosophy above rationalism and empiricism,[32]

---

[31] WSJ, 'Greenspan Testimony on Sources of Financial Crisis', *The Wall Street Journal*, 23 October 2008, https://www.wsj.com/articles/BL-REB-2187, italics are mine.
[32] Dieter Henrich shows that there are two ideas concerning the foundation of ethics originating from Thomas Hobbes, namely the rational ethics of Clarke, Wollaston and Wolff, and the moral-sense philosophy of Shaftesbury, Hutcheson and Butler. The presuppositions formulated by Wolff, Crusius and Hutcheson constitute the context of Kant's development of ethics, and this context led Kant to the discovery of the formula of the categorical imperative as early as 1765, see Dieter Henrich, *The Unity of Reason: Essays on Kant's Philosophy* (Cambridge, MA: Harvard University Press, 1994), 67–72. Hutcheson's theory of moral sense (as it is often claimed to have inherited from Shaftesbury, though it is also claimed that Shaftesbury's ethical theory is closer to the rationalists than to the empiricists) is the precursor to Hume's moral sentimentalism, see Stephen Darwell, *Modern Moral Philosophy: From Grotius to Kant* (Cambridge: Cambridge University Press, 2023), 140.

and indeed he condemns the employments of reason which are either technically or empirically determined; instead, Kant suggests that practical reason should legislate by itself.[33]

We will return to the Kant machine in order to understand how it works in this context. Kant's transcendental philosophy, as we have seen, is an alternative to rationalism as well as to empiricism. Kant leaves the power of judgement to reason itself without it being guided or obliged by any external force or empirical knowledge. The Kantian machine, in this way, avoids the problem of the Humean machine regarding the vulnerability of causal laws derived from empirical experience. Kantian morality is, first of all, *non-analytic* and, second, *non-empirical*. It is not analytical since a general law is not given in advance and not demonstratable, one which, if present, could guide all human actions just as physical laws do to nature (we recall the rationalist teaching such as Wolff's that morality could be proved through demonstration); it is also not empirical because a moral judgement should be independent of empirical experience, which cannot guarantee the validity of the universal. Kantian morality is a particular kind of algorithm, to which Kant gives the name the categorical imperative. For Kant, the highest good (*summum bonum*) means a world in which everyone behaves according to the categorical imperative, hence *summum* carries more the meaning of *consummatum* (completion) than *supremum* (supreme). We could imagine a scenario in which every individual is an algorithm capable of moral reflective judgement; each algorithm, or what Kant calls 'each rational being in the world',[34] aims at the universal just as a moral agent aims at its own moral perfection. How can this be achievable? What might be the 'technical procedure'[35] of the categorical imperative?

In the *Critique of Practical Reason*, the heuristic of the Categorical Imperative remained obscure beyond the command of universalization. It is only in the *Critique of Judgment* that the reflective nature of moral judgement is clarified, namely, through the operation of reflective judgement. Reflective judgement is that which connects both aesthetic and teleological judgements, and also that which remains central but obscure in moral judgements. In §59 'Beauty as the Symbol of Morality', Kant spells out the *analogy* between the beautiful and the moral. This analogy is significant because aesthetic judgement intervenes in the

---

[33] Gilles Deleuze, *Kant's Critical Philosophy*, trans. Hugh Tomlinson and Barbara Habberjam (London: The Athlone Press, 1984), 37.
[34] Kant, *Critique of Judgment*, §87, 278; Ak. 5:449.
[35] A term hinted at by Kant in the first introduction to the *Critique of Judgment*, and later formulated by Gerhard Lehmann.

faculty of feeling and moral judgements intervene in the faculty of desire, namely two tribunals of a different nature; if an analogy could be established between them, it means that they share something in common. But to proceed, we should first return to §17 where Kant gives us a formal definition of beauty, namely 'Beauty is the form of purposiveness in an object, so far as this is perceived in it apart from the representation of an end'.[36] Beauty here doesn't refer directly to the object, for example, its representation but rather the representation of the end; such an end is only conceivable through subjective reflective judgement. Kant deviates from modern logicians who oppose the symbol to an intuitive mode of representation; instead, he returns the symbol to a form of intuition juxtaposing it to that of schemata. Schemata means direct presentations of the concept, while symbols mean indirect presentations. Symbols function according to analogies, namely first applying the concept of an object of sensuous intuition A, and second, applying the rules of its reflection upon the intuition of A to B, of which A is a symbol.[37] Beauty as the symbol of morality means that the way beauty is reflectively judged is analogical to that of morality, with the difference that they operate on two different sets of registers. According to §59 of the *Critique of Judgment*, we can summarize the analogy in the following four points:

1. The pleasure of the beautiful, operates reflectively in intuition; the pleasure of the moral, operates reflectively in the concept.
2. The beautiful pleases by negating all interests (pleasure without interest), the moral pleases by negating interests 'antecedent to the judgement upon the delight.'
3. The beautiful is judged by the freedom of imagination in conforming to law; the moral is judged by the freedom of the will.
4. The judgement of the beautiful is according to the subjective principle; the moral according to objective principle.[38]

The pleasure that is proper to aesthetic judgement is not an agreement [*consensus*]; that is to say, it does not function in the manner that the sensible is subsumed under rational principles – a task Alexander Baumgarten, the 'admirable analytical thinker' (A21/B36), set himself;[39] nor is it a return to the

---

[36] Kant, *Critique of Judgment*, 66; Ak. 5:236.
[37] Kant, *Critique of Judgment*, 179; Ak. 5:351–2; we have discussed Kant's analogical method in Chapter 1 against the backdrop of his own criticism of Herder's use of analogy.
[38] Kant, *Critique of Judgment*, 181; Ak. 5:354.
[39] Baumgarten even though recognizes that aesthetics belongs to the 'inferior cognition', he still wants to elevate its rank by making it analogous to reason. Making aesthetics a science is also about discovering rational principles that govern sensory cognition, for example, beauty (*pulcritudo*) means the perfection of sensible knowledge, determined by the harmony of thoughts (*consensus*

inexplicability of the workings of taste, expressed in the early seventeenth-century French saying '*je ne sais quoi*'.⁴⁰ What Kant presents here as a resolution to the aporia of aesthetic judgement is analogous to that of moral judgement. This by no means claims that the aesthetic is the same as the moral; they belong to different faculties and operate on different planes. The aesthetic idea is an *inexponible* representation of the imagination, and the rational idea is the *indemonstrable* concept of reason.⁴¹ An analogy is not a claim of identity but rather a claim of comparable structure and operation, as already discussed in Chapter 1. Even though Kant points out their symetrical differences, that is, the intuition/imagination/subjective principle versus the concept/will/objective principle;⁴² yet more importantly, they share the same structure and operation. Gerhard Lehmann in an article titled 'Die Technik der Natur' opposes what Kant called technical practice [*Technische Praktik*], or what Kant himself calls 'technical-practical reason') to natural technics [*natürliche Technik*].⁴³ The technical practice contains the hypothetical imperative in its two forms, that is, technical imperative (e.g. rules of skill) and pragmatic imperative (e.g. counsels of prudence). The difference between technical practice and natural technics could be summarized in Lehmann's own words: 'If technical practice is the *conscious realization* of purposes, natural technique is the *unconscious representation* of purposes in nature'.⁴⁴ Lehmann added that there is an intermediate category, namely, the work of art. The work of art belongs to technical practice, yet it is analogous to nature: 'works of art appear as natural products, and organic bodies as works of art'.⁴⁵ This connection, as suggested by Lehmann, is made possible by what Kant calls the technics of judgement [*Technik der Urteilskraft*], a concept developed in the first introduction to the third *Critique*, which Kant didn't publish himself. What consists in this technical procedure [*technisches Verfahren*] of judgement? Lehmann suggests that it functions 'insofar as nature

---

cogitationum), harmony of order (*consensus ordinis*) and harmony of signs (*consensus signorum*). See Alexander Baumgarten, *Aesthetica* (Latin-German) (Hamburg: Felix Meiner), 2007, §15–20.

⁴⁰ See Hui, *Art and Cosmotechnics*, §15 'The Realm of the Noumenon'.

⁴¹ Kant, *Critique of Judgment*, 170; Ak. 5:342.

⁴² It is, however, doubtful if the judgement of taste is in reflective intuition only, because in §56 on the antinomy of the judgement of taste, Kant resolves the antinomy by telling us that it is based on a concept, which is not determinative; instead, it is the transcendental rational concept of the supersensible. If we understand what he says literally, then the beautiful is not to be found in the reflective intuition alone. See Kant, *Critique of Judgment*, §57, 167; Ak. 5:339.

⁴³ Gerhard Lehmann, 'Technik der Natur', in *Beiträge zur Geschichte und Interpretation der Philosophie Kants* (Berlin: De Gruyter, 1969), 291.

⁴⁴ Lehmann, 'Technik der Natur', 291, 'Ist die technische Praktik bewußte Zweckverwirklichung, so ist die natürliche Technik unbewußte Zweckdarstellung in der Natur'.

⁴⁵ Lehmann, 'Technik der Natur', 291, 'Kunstwerke erscheinen als Naturprodukte und organische Körper als Kunstwerke'.

exhibits the same traits of plasticity, inventiveness, and purposive activity that characterize our (reflective) judgement'.⁴⁶ Besides the reflective judgement, the other important element is holistic structure [*ganzheitliche Struktur*].⁴⁷ We might say, in the spirit of Simondon (though not in Kant's own exact wording), that they are analogical in terms of their *reflective operation* (recursion) and *organic structure* (parts and whole) instead of their identity.

This is how Kant's elaboration of the reflective judgement in the third *Critique* fills out the gap left in the second *Critique*, namely, how synthetic moral judgements are a priori possible. The analogy between the beautiful and the moral alludes to the centrality of reflective judgement, or more precisely, the reflective operation, which allows a progressive movement towards the universal. It is not a mere reflection, but a reflection that negates empirical inclinations which are merely agreeable or unexamined.⁴⁸ Where will the judgement land? Alexandre Kojève clearly saw the relation between subjective reflective judgement and moral judgement, since both of them look for a subjective certainty instead of truth as an exact and definite destination:

> It [Kantian Theology] is now also founded on and by the Teleology of the third Critique. Just like 'Moral Faith,' this 'Teleology' is only a subjective Certainty and not a Truth. But it has the enormous advantage of being able to derive its Meaning and thus its 'evidence' from ordinary sensible Experience, that is, in our terminology, from Perception. And this is how the third *Critique* fills the gap that we noted in the first draft of the Kantian System and that Kant himself must have eventually noticed.⁴⁹

Kojève understands that both teleology and morality couldn't be approached in the discursive mode of truth, but only in the mode of 'as if'.⁵⁰ The 'as if' mode, whether moral or aesthetic, requires *faith*. We could align Kojève's interpretation with our own: when the Kantian system moves out of the discursive mode of truth to the mode of 'as if', the System sketched in the first *Critique* is expanded beyond the island of pure theoretical reason driven by other aims and other uses

---

⁴⁶ Lehmann, 'Technik der Natur', 291–2.
⁴⁷ Lehmann, 'Technik der Natur', 292.
⁴⁸ In the *Opus Postumum*, Kant points out that for aesthetic determination, pleasure comes before the law; and for moral determination, pleasure comes after the law, that is, the categorical imperative, see Kant, *Ak.22*, 1 Convolut, XII Bogen, Seite 1.
⁴⁹ Alexandre Kojève, *Kant* (Paris: Gallimard, 1973), 84.
⁵⁰ Kojève, *Kant*, 139, 'Kant refuse d' 'appliquer' discursivement les Catégories à la chose-en-soi *dans le mode de la Vérité*. Mais il se réserve le droit (dont il se sert dans la *troisième Critique* et dans la 'Partie pratique de sa Philosophie' de les y 'appliquer' *dans le mode de Comme-si*' (Italics are original).

of reason.[51] In so doing, Kant was under pressure to formulate the heuristic of the mode of 'as if' beyond a general definition of the regulative principle.

Back to the Kant machine, if we follow our claim on the centrality of reflective judgement in Kant's philosophy, it might suggest that, given a well-calibrated algorithm, the recursive operation of computation machines has the potential to move towards the direction Kant hinted at for the transcendental system. Such speculation was not a possibility in the era of Vaucanson's automata, since their reasoning remained too linear to articulate good and evil; in critical philosophy, the notion of 'system' was distinguished from mere mechanism and used as a totalizing 'framework' to articulate good and evil.[52] In this sense, we can fully understand Kant's criticism against Vaucanson's automata in the second *Critique*, though we also have to recognize that it is not valid to reuse it against machines today. The development of recursive machines and their assimilation of the notion of system presents a significant advancement. A machine, in comparison with a human being, is able to perform reflections without getting tired as long as there is an infinite electricity supply and infinite memory and storage, like the Turing machine. However, could such a machine ever arrive at Kantian morality?

If the moral principle of the machine were empiricism, then it could, *at most*, arrive at a decision regarding the *most agreeable*. Let us revisit the famous trolley problem: as a driver, either you do nothing and let the trolley kill five people passing by on the track, or you divert the trolley to the side track and kill one person. Which is more moral than the other? The Humean moral machine might, within seconds, be able to derive a response from experience (or data), which shows the average result evaluated according to different parameters defined by, for example, region, religion, economy, background of the victims, compensation policies of the insurance companies, legal consequences and so on, which couldn't be done by the human mind within seconds. The Kantian moral machine doesn't follow empirical inclination as defined by norms; indeed,

---

[51] As Kant claims that the first *Critique* is a 'treatise on the method' (B xxii), and not exactly a system of transcendental philosophy.

[52] We are tempted to suggest that Kant uses system to articulate the transcendental principle of the good, while Schelling uses system to articulate the transcendental principle of evil. For Kant, freedom is often considered as the capability for good; for Schelling, it is the capability of both good and evil. For Schelling, evil cannot be placed outside the system; that is, it doesn't mean that outside the system is good or evil, instead, one can only understand evil within the system, namely a moment of perversion in the system, see F. W. J. Schelling, *Philosophical Investigations into the Essence of Human Freedom*, trans. Jeff Love and Johannes Schmidt (Albany, NY: State University of New York, 2006). However, 'framework' might not be the best word to describe the system, as Heidegger would insist, and it is more appropriate to call the system 'the totality of Being in the totality of its truth and the history of the truth', see Martin Heidegger, *Schelling's Treatise on the Essence of Human Freedom*, trans. Joan Stambaugh (Athens, OH: Ohio University Press, 1985), 48.

it refuses it. Instead, norms should first be negatively examined according to whether they are universal; the moral agent's own concrete situation will have to be taken into account, for example, whether it is a more universal decision to choose to save one of their own acquaintances than to kill five strangers.

This does not mean that the categorical imperative acts independently from the empirical. While the Kantian machine discriminates the transcendental from the empirical, it cannot bypass the empirical. Kant knew too well that transcendental laws are empty without empirical facts; in the case of the transcendental deduction of the categories, facts are used to verify the deduction; in the case of moral laws which cannot be transcendentally deduced, empirical facts are the source of contingency which motivates the movement towards the universal. In other words, without the empirical and its inclinations, the machine cannot move forward; namely, it stagnates.[53] The empirical is not that which determines, but rather it is recursively tested by the machine. What can we infer from this? The Kantian moral machine is opposed to the Humean machine which is the paradigm (if we speak with Thomas Kuhn here) of current artificial intelligence; at the same time, the Kantian machine is also paradoxically close to it, since the recursive algorithm makes the moral reflective judgement a concrete possibility – namely, an agent, when well programmed, might be able to negate empirical inclinations and arrive at a law free from non-universalizable desires and interests. In this sense, machines might even possess a higher degree of 'freedom' than the human being because a machine can automatize reflections. This renders the classical distinction between automation and autonomy less self-evident or even increasingly blurred. It gives the impression that a formalization of a Kantian moral machine is not only possible but also desirable. Indeed, some authors might well imagine building a database of categorical imperatives so that the machine can exclude the non-categorical

---

[53] Here we encounter a tension in Kant's writing regarding the relation between anthropology and moral metaphysics. In Kant's earlier lectures (1770s) on anthropology, he suggests that morality cannot exist without anthropology and that a practical philosophy without anthropology is merely speculative (*Ak.* 27: 244), while in his later work on moral metaphysics (i.e. *Groundwork of the Metaphysics of Morals* (1785)), Kant considered anthropology as an empirical psychology and was looking for a 'pure moral philosophy, completely cleansed of everything that may be empirical and that belongs to anthropology' (*Ak.* 4: 388f). Retrospectively, what Kant describes as the faculty of desire in *Anthropology from a Pragmatic Point of View*, trans. Robert B. Louden (Cambridge: Cambridge University Press, 2006) is largely empirical, where he talks about affects, fear and so on; and it ceases to be the case in the *Critique of Practical Reason*, where practical reason becomes dominant and negates empirical inclinations. It seems that there is a sharp detachment between anthropology and moral metaphysics, as Manfred Kuehn noticed in the 'Introduction' to *Anthropology from a Pragmatic Point of View* (xx–xxi); however, without the empirical, the categorical imperative could hardly operate.

imperatives;[54] however, it would appear contradictory to formulate a set of rules under the name categorical imperative, since by doing so, they might be simply prescriptions. Alternatively, one might want to formulate the categorical imperative as Kant himself did and turn it into an algorithm, as described above. The challenge lies then in its realization because it is not a prescription that reason has to execute but a process of self-legislation called upon by duty, by the constrain reason places upon our individual, subjective will. It is also here that the Kantian machine dramatically encounters Turing's halting problem and Gödel's Incompleteness Theorem. In his 1936 paper 'On Computable Numbers, with an Application to the *Entscheidungsproblem*',[55] Turing envisioned a universal machine (with an infinite tape for memory) capable of simulating any other Turing machine. The halting problem arises when there is no general algorithm that can determine, for every possible input, whether a given programme will eventually halt or run forever. In other words, it is undecidable whether certain programmes will stop. As a result, a machine may keep running indefinitely without any means of knowing in advance if it should stop. The Turing machine will have to distinguish the computable from the incomputable, because it has only *one* faculty determined by computability. Computability, in this context, means that for any given natural number – regardless of its size – there exists an algorithm that can generate it in a finite number of steps. If no such algorithm can be found, the number is considered incomputable. This notion connects back to our earlier discussion of Solomonoff's algorithmic information theory, which highlights the limits of compressibility and algorithmic generation; in other words, data that cannot be compressed is "algorithmically irreducible or structurally random".[56] In contrast, the Kantian machine has three faculties: the faculty of cognition, the faculty of desire and the faculty of feeling.[57] Each

---

[54] See Thomas M. Powers, 'Machines and Moral Reasoning' (2009), https://philosophynow.org/issues/72/Machines_and_Moral_Reasoning, where the author tried to imagine the implementation of a Kantian moral machine, 'suppose we could begin with one universal law and then build the database of permissible maxims by an iterative process, generating them from the one law we had. Once we had a large enough database we could instruct the computer to act on the following rule: 'Only do action a if it appears in the database of permissible maxims''. We can hardly take it seriously because, first, the inclusion of the categorical imperative is not possible, since it is a maxim of universalizing but neither a rule nor mathematical induction; therefore, it is never complete. Second, the exclusion of non-categorical imperatives only excludes certain searching heuristics; it doesn't mean that it is moving towards the universal through such an exclusion.

[55] The *Entscheidungsproblem* of David Hilbert asks whether there is a mechanical procedure (algorithm) that can determine, for any given mathematical statement, whether that statement is true or false within a formal system.

[56] Gregory Chaitin, "An Algorithmic God," *Inference: International Review of Science*, 1,No.4 (October 2015), https://inference-review.com/article/an-algorithmic-god#

[57] Kant's multiple faculties doctrine distinguishes him from the one source doctrine of philosophers such as Christian Wolff and William Wollaston.

faculty involves a distinct form of legislation, which could be roughly simplified as follows: understanding legislates for cognition through a priori categories, reason legislates for morality by determining the moral law, and judgement governs aesthetic experience through the principle of purposiveness, which gives rise to aesthetic common sense [*sensus communis*]. While these faculties are distinct, they remain interconnected rather than mechanically separate, with reason playing an omnipresent yet varying role across them.

One could draw an affinity between the Turing machine and the faculty of cognition because both of them only function within a boundary that decides on the validity of knowledge. The faculty of cognition is not able to deal with the incomputable since the latter is supersensible [*übersinnlich*] and therefore cannot be reduced to an object of experience. In Kant, we can identify two ways of handling the 'incomputable', one is exemplified by the sublime, and the other by the beautiful and the moral. In the case of the sublime, we can use the example of the pyramid given by Kant in the *Critique of Judgment* – an example he borrowed from the orientalist Claude-Étienne Savary. In encountering a pyramid, when we are too close to it, our gaze always rests on successive apprehensions [*Auffassung*] without being able to comprehend [*zusammenfassen*] the pyramid as a unity.[58] Reason is this force that interrupts and imposes its violence on the imagination to enforce a halting status in order to allow the subject to comprehend its own limit. The same goes for the dynamic sublime, in which the machine is overwhelmed by the immeasurability and uncontrollability of the data that it has to process – here, horror is felt, and respect [*Achtung*] emerges.

We have to remind ourselves that Kant never saw a pyramid; indeed, he never travelled to Egypt (or very far at all), he might only have encountered it in books or drawings; photography of course not being available in the eighteenth century. Kant performed a thought experiment characterized by an infinite looping, surprising himself with the incomputable; this led to the evidence of a different faculty at work and a different realm other than that of the phenomenon. Even though on several occasions Turing insists that the existence of the incomputable (which was analysed in the same period by Gödel, Church and Kleene) doesn't imply that machines don't have intelligence, he still limited himself to the faculty of cognition (it should be noted, though, that Turing wanted to address telepathy, clairvoyance, precognition and the psycho-kinesis of machines; he stopped there by saying that he would have to tighten up the imitation game

---

[58] Kant, *Critique of Judgement*, §26, 82–3; Ak. 5:252.

were telepathy admitted).[59] Kant refuses to reduce feeling and morality to the natural sciences. Consequently, he also sets boundaries for science, which are considered as an island 'surrounded by a vast and stormy ocean, where illusion properly resides and many fog banks and much fast-melting ice feign new-found lands'.[60] Contrary to the understanding, the faculty of desire and the faculty of feeling are capable of dealing with the supersensible. One should, therefore, be convinced that Kant very well knows the halting problem Turing had to confront. Now we can examine the second way of handling the halting problem, exemplified by that of the moral. It is more complex than the beautiful we examined earlier because it also involves the conflicts of reason, and it also shows us the second (or the third) sense of Kant's epigenesis of reason, even though the term 'epigenesis' is absent in the second critique. To engage with the supersensible – here understood as the moral realm – reason has to undergo a process of expansion so that the apparent contradiction between theoretical and practical reason could be resolved through *compromise*. We might, therefore, make the following claim:

1) Reason is epigenetic, because it is always under pressure of expansion [*Erweiterung*] due to the incompatibility of theoretical and practical reason; in so doing, it has to adjust itself in order not to contradict itself.

The epigenesis of reason is not empirical, as we endeavoured to show in the previous chapter; nor does it mean the plasticity of the brain or the mind.[61] It rather means that reason has to undergo a journey of self-discovery: and in such a process, it has to understand its limits while cautiously expanding itself beyond these boundaries without falling into fanaticism – this is also the moment when the Kantian antinomy becomes compatible with Hegelian dialectics, as the resolution of the antinomy entails the expansion of reason. While the second *Critique* didn't use the word epigenesis, one could, nevertheless, still trace its significance in what Kant calls the expansion [*Erweiterung*] of reason.[62] The occasion when Kant talks about the expansion of reason is in the section of the

---

[59] Turing, 'Computational Machinery and Intelligence', in *The Essential Turing*, 458.
[60] Kant, *Critique of Pure Reason*, B295.
[61] This doesn't mean that plasticity makes no sense; indeed, when we consider the 'geological formation' of the categories in understanding, as we have shown in Chapter 1, one has to admit a certain sense of plasticity. However, as we are trying to show in this chapter, what Kant means by epigenesis is far beyond the plasticity of the brain; it demands a radical expansion of reason beyond its comfort zone.
[62] Susan Neiman in *The Unity of Reason: Reading Kant* (Oxford: Oxford University Press, 1994) raised a very important question, namely, 'How should we explain the fact that no full-length study has been devoted to Kant's conception of reason?' (3). The difficulty is that there is no reason as such, but rather an epigenesis of reason which took Kant a long time to spell out systematically, that is to say, without contradiction.

second *Critique* entitled 'How it is possible to think an expansion of pure reason for practical aim without thereby also expanding its cognition as speculative? [*Wie eine Erweiterung der reinen Vernunft, in praktischer Absicht, ohne damit ihr Erkenntnis, als spekulativ, zugleich zu erweitern, zu denken möglich sei?*]'. What is at stake in this section is a discussion of the recognition of the theoretically non-demonstrable entities (or ideas) such as God, Freedom and the immortal Soul, a demonstration that theoretical reason could not offer; however, for *practical* purposes, reason has to postulate their existence, which cannot be informed by any empirical evidence and knowledge.[63] The expansion of reason is not because of a preformationist growth, but rather, reason is forced to go beyond its comfort zone and to recognize the existence of entities that it cannot prove, yet without which it cannot operate:[64]

> By this, then, the theoretical cognition of pure reason does of course acquire an increase [*Zuwachs*], which however consists merely in this: that those concepts, which are otherwise problematic (merely thinkable), are now assertorically declared to be concepts to which objects actually belong, because practical reason unavoidably requires the existence of these for the possibility of its object, the highest Good, which moreover is absolutely necessary practically, and theoretical reason is thereby entitled to presuppose them . . . this expansion [*Erweiterung*] of theoretical reason is not an expansion of speculation, i.e. no positive use [*nunmehr einen positiven Gebrauch*] can now be made of it for a theoretical aim.[65]

The incompatibility between theoretical-speculative reason and practical-moral reason is, in fact, generalized in all antinomies, which reveals the non-triviality of reason and the aporetic nature of judgement.[66] This incompatibility is what Simondon would call disparity, the condition of individuation; for example, the two images received by the retina are incompatible, namely, they are two distinct

---

[63] Here one may identify a rather intriguing question that violates our everyday language, namely, how to postulate a fact? Because the moral law is not an empirical fact, but a transcendental fact, or the *fact of reason*, at the same time, it is also postulated.

[64] One may want to raise the following question: Is Kant not a pragmatist? From the outset, Kant wants to complete his system with postulates which he cannot prove; therefore, it might give the impression of a pragmatist approach. However, the pragmatists, William James in particular, determine something as being true (e.g. the existence of God) according to the effect of such a belief, that is, if it is good for life, see William James, *Pragmatism: A New Name for Some Old Ways of Thinking* (Cambridge, MA: Harvard University Press, 1907), 42; Kant sees it more as a functional necessity of reason regardless of its effect.

[65] Kant, *Critique of Practical Reason*, 171–1; Ak. 5:134–5.

[66] The aporia of judgement is a theme explored by Howard Caygill, *Art of Judgment* (Oxford: Blackwell, 1989); instead of following philosophers such as Jean-François Lyotard who read the third *Critique* as the exposition of a system failure in which pleasure couldn't be brought under judgement, Caygill shows that reason finds its pleasure in the aporia of judgement.

images; however, it is precisely this incompatibility that triggers an individuation to take place in order to resolve the excessive tensions that we are able to perceive one unified and calibrated image. The history of philosophy could also be seen as a history of the expansion of reason, in which older systems are surpassed and new generalizations are developed in order to accommodate the particular and the universal.[67] In our context, the Kantian morality implies an expansion of reason (beyond the confines of theoretical-speculative reason), namely, the recognition of the supersensible beings, such as the existence of God and the immortal Soul, something that theoretical reason cannot prove and admit with ease. However, it is necessary to recognize them from a practical aim; therefore, it is a 'pure practical rational belief', a 'taking-to-be-true' [*Fürwahrhalten*].[68] Here lies an important epistemological grounding in Kant's philosophical system. We are not talking about system A or system B, but rather *System* in general. In so far as we want to think systemically, there is virtually nothing outside it; the *System* contains rational, irrational and non-rational beings. While the rational is opposed to the irrational, it would be a mistake to reduce the non-rational to the irrational.[69] The non-rational entities or ideas (such as Freedom and God) which cannot be demonstrated in the empirical world also find their place in the *System* if they can serve the purpose of regulating and elevating human beings towards an end where nature and freedom meet.[70]

Given that the categorical imperative consists of recursive movements, Kant was aware that it couldn't arrive at an exact universal, and for two reasons. First, such a universal, even though it has objective existence, is not a thing, but rather 'unthinged' (*unbedingt, das Unbedingte* is often translated as the Absolute; that is, the Absolute is that which cannot be reduced to a thing and without condition). Therefore, we cannot arrive at it as truth but only approximate it in terms of the 'as if'. This 'as if' can carry a double meaning here: first, as stated above, we cannot exactly know what it is; second, every judgement could err, since deciding whether it is right or wrong belongs to the understanding's objective judgement; nevertheless, it demands *belief*. Indeed, one can at least know if one truly believes in the judgement or whether one merely pretends to do so – thus

---

[67] And in this sense philosophy is speculative in nature as Whitehead claims, see Alfred North Whitehead, *Process and Reality*, ed. D. R. Griffin and D. W. Sherburne (New York: Free Press, 1978), Chapter 1 'Speculative Philosophy'.
[68] Kant, *Ak*. 5:144, 142; also quoted by Lara Ostaric, *The Critique of Judgment and the Unity of Kant's Critical System* (Cambridge: Cambridge University Press, 2023), 60.
[69] For a more elaborated discussion on the rational, irrational and non-rational, please see Yuk Hui, *Art and Cosmotechnics* (Minneapolis, MN: University of Minnesota Press, 2021).
[70] *Art and Cosmotechnics* raises the question of how to position the non-rational within the conceptualization of the relation between art and technology.

the moral force of duty is implied.[71] Second, this algorithm's recursive operation is endless – this is the reason that Kant claims that for morality to be possible, one should postulate the existence of the immortal soul.[72] Hence our second claim, that:

2) The epigenesis of reason has to take the risk of recognizing the objective existence of the thing-in-itself, God, the immortal Soul and Freedom without being able to demonstrate their existence, while at the same time, it cannot operate without these postulates.

The postulate concerning the existence of God remains royal to the philosophical tradition that posits God on cosmological grounds, for without the creation and perfection of God, the cosmos would not be possible. The postulate concerning the existence of the immortal soul is more intriguing here because we encounter the halting problem for arriving at the highest Good. To reiterate, Kant's concept of freedom means the capacity to act rationally against empirical inclinations which cannot be universalized (and it would be an impasse to the highest Good). In the world of the highest Good that Kant proposed, it is a programme in which every algorithm, considered as a rational agent, is evaluating the universal ceaselessly. While Kant knows that it is not possible for one to be certain that he or she performs the duty selfishly,[73] he requires us to use our reason to examine these empirical inclinations, which sometimes also appear as moral norms. The highest Good is therefore a collective Good, but also the Good that could only be collectively realized. There is no guarantee when exactly the highest Good will be reached, though one can be sure that arriving at it will take much longer than one's own life. Therefore, for the highest Good to be realizable, one should expect that it will take an indefinite amount of time since no one knows when exactly it will happen. In view of this indefinite and possibly infinite waiting, the

---

[71] This second point is emphasized in Kant, 'On the Miscarriage of all Philosophical Trials in Theodicy', in *Religion within the Boundaries of Mere Reason and Other Writings*, trans. Allen Wood and George di Giovanni (Cambridge: Cambridge University Press, 1998), 27; *Ak.* 8:268, a paragraph earlier Kant reminds us that the principal requirement of faith is sincerity.

[72] In the *Critique of Pure Reason*, A338, B396 footnote 222, God, freedom and immortality are said to be the only three essential ideas of metaphysics; they form a synthetic order, namely the first concepts will lead to the third as conclusion; but a systematic presentation will have to reverse this synthetic order into an analytic order.

[73] This is also an argument which Kant used to refuse the accusation of Christian Garve that theory is separated from practice, such as the desire of happiness is separated from performing duty, the head from the heart. Kant's point is not that one can be sure of performing one's duty selflessly, but without the guidance of duty, one is lost in the satisfaction of particular desires. Kant wants to show that not only is theory not inferior to practice but also practice alone cannot lead to any end beyond particular desires, see Kant 'On the common saying: That may be correct in theory, but it is of no use in practice', in Immanuel Kant, *Practical Philosophy*, trans. Mary J. Gregor (Cambridge: Cambridge University Press, 1999), 286; *Ak.* 8: 284.

immortal soul has to be postulated as the condition of arriving at the highest good.

> Complete adequacy of the will to the moral law, however, is *holiness*, a perfection of which no rational being in the world of sense is capable at any point of time in his existence. Since this adequacy is nonetheless demanded as practically necessary, it can be encountered only in a progression proceeding *ad infinitum* toward that complete adequacy; and according to principles of pure practical reason it is necessary to assume such a practical advance as the real object of our will.[74]

In other words, even though Kant anticipated the halting problem, he didn't force the programme to terminate as in the case of the sublime. Instead, Kant grants the incomputable a higher status and rationalizes the incomputable by extending the time of computation to *ad infinitum*. If the norm itself is doubtful, it will have to search for what could be *more* moral and just. The consciousness of the moral law, however, belongs to a different kind of fact; it is not an empirical fact, but rather a fact of pure reason. Since it is a fact of reason, this is *not* an error; however, humans will never be able to realize it *in actu* or *in concreto*. In this case, it is also an ideal of pure reason, one which we can only approximate, 'as if' there is an end.

Morality for Kant is incomputable, or better incalculable since it is beyond the faculty of cognition.[75] Now, we have to ask, given that morality is incalculable, what does it mean to our initial question of whether machines are capable of being moral. If the essence of machines is calculability, then one could conclude that it is impossible for artificial intelligence to become moral, because it is very likely to end up in infinite looping without knowing when to halt. AI can treat concepts like God, Freedom and the immortal Soul as symbols, just as one could give the symbol ∞ to infinity without being able to count it, distinguishing each of them based on their spellings.[76] However, it cannot comprehend the deeper meanings of these concepts beyond their numerical or alphabetic representations, which are then subsumed to the calculation of probabilities. It is a different kind of 'paradox of mechanisation', which Haugland talked about, and was mentioned in Chapter 1; because it is not that the machine cannot understand the semantic meaning of the term (in so far as we understand that the meaning of the term is determined by other terms in the same sentence,

---

[74] Kant, *Critique of Practical Reason*, 155; Ak. 5:122.
[75] Computability is still a mathematical question; incalculability means it cannot be thought of mathematically.
[76] This is nominalism in practice, as Locke would have insisted.

i.e. its use), but rather it doesn't understand the meaning of the meaning of the term. Beyond the distinction between the thing and its representation, the more fundamental issue in our context is the question of time. Even though a great programmer might unconsciously presuppose the existence of God or perform God's task like a genius, such as the mathematician and another key figure in algorithmic information theory Gregory Chaitin has expressed that the best algorithms should have the quality of Leibniz's best of all possible worlds chosen by God (i.e. simplest in hypothesis and richest in phenomena),[77] he or she cannot entertain an *ad infinitum* time of executing the algorithm. The algorithm can continue to operate recursively, but since it cannot be terminated, the judgement will be forever suspended.

Back to the question of alignment which we contested in the beginning, we can say that the superaligned machine is not a moral machine, but rather one that is subordinated to empirical norms; being moral in this sense only means computing and following norms. By collecting and analysing data, it is able to arrive at a set of norms, and it is able to make subsequent decisions based on these norms; however, by doing so, it doesn't exceed the limit of an empirical machine. Superalignment is only proof that machines *cannot* be moral since they are bound by social norms. A misaligned machine is either one that fails to calculate the social norms due to a lack of data, or one that fails to halt.

§6. The moral, the teleological and the technological

Given the similarity between the teleomechanism in the third *Critique* and contemporary computational machines, we have been tempted to ask if a moral machine is possible at all; however, we can only arrive at the conclusion that it is impossible. And given that we have already examined the analogy between the beautiful and the moral, we may also logically refuse that an AI painter, in its current form, would be capable of creating a *truly beautiful* painting, since it can only either follow established norms (e.g. the style of Van Gogh) or inductively predict the best next pictorial element to appear. The work produced by AI carries no necessity but only probability – one could decompose Kandinsky's

---

[77] G. W. Leibniz, *Discourse on Metaphysics and Other Essays*, trans. Daniel Garber and Roger Ariew (Indianapolis, IN: Hackett, 1989), 39: 'God has chosen the most perfect world, that is, the one which is at the same time the simplest in hypotheses and the richest in phenomena, as might be a line in geometry whose construction is easy and whose properties and effects are extremely remarkable and widespread'. Also cited by Gregory Chaitin, 'Leibniz, Information, Math and Physics', 2005, http://arxiv.org/abs/math/0306303.

abstract paintings, for example Composition (II), into various figural elements such as circles, triangles and retangles, and colors, then reassemble them according to different permutations by putting the figural elements at different places on the canvas with a nuanced color. No matter how similar they look like to Kandinsky's paintings, this could hardly be called creativity. Artistic creativity, by contrast, is always haunted by contingency and must culminate in an affirmation of necessity – as in Beethoven's String Quartet No. 16, whose fourth movement begins with the question 'Muss es sein?' and answers decisively: 'Es muss sein!' However, even though we are convinced that the machine cannot judge what is beautiful and is not capable of being moral, we still have to ask what the role of the machine is in the pursuit of creativity and morality. To put the question in a different way, we might want to ask what is the purposiveness of automation? Automation is often associated with an external purposiveness (or a 'relative purposiveness'[78]); that is to say, it is driven by a utilitarian reason. We can use ChatGPT to translate a text or to inquire how a sentence could be differently expressed. However, this is only an external purposiveness since it is driven not by the machine itself but rather by something outside of the condition of existence of the machine. Internal purposiveness is something else; it means the autonomy of the being in question. We don't know the purposiveness of the existence of this or that monkey; it is, for sure, not for our pleasure or for any medical experiment; however, in the monkey, there is a purposiveness of survival that constantly resists the rapid dissipation of energy, since the latter means moving towards death. We could also talk about another purposiveness, which is the purposiveness of nature itself, what Kant calls the end of nature; we don't really know what it is despite the fact that, according to the second law of thermodynamics, we are witnessing its disintegration. However, maybe only when a total disintegration arrives will we know its purposiveness. The natural end can only be thought of in the mode of 'as if' and not in the mode of truth, as we have seen above. Nevertheless, the question still remains: what is nature's end, even if it could only be thought of in the mode of the 'as if'?

It must be noted that Kant did not subscribe to the theory that God designs the world. Besides rejecting theism, he also refuses both idealism and realism of natural ends, or put differently, Spinoza's fatalism and Herder's vitalist pantheism.[79] Realism believes that it is possible to find a cause operating intentionally and consequently falls back on hylozoism, attributing the logic of the living to matter,

---

[78] Kant, *Critique of Judgment*, §63; Ak. 5:377.
[79] John Zammito, *The Genesis of Kant's Critique of Judgment* (Chicago, IL: The University of Chicago Press, 1992), 230.

while Kant believes that 'the possibility of a living matter is quite inconceivable';[80] idealism holds the view that nature is without design; therefore, it subordinates itself to the accidentalism of atomism and the fatalism of Spinozism. Kant criticized that Spinoza 'holds the view that there is a unity of ground', and 'rejects the unity of end' which meant that 'consequently, he also robbed away contingency, without which no unity of end is thinkable'.[81] This criticism demands further qualification.[82] By saying that Spinoza rejects the 'unity of end', Kant means that Spinoza's philosophy doesn't give place to a teleology which is not based on rationalist analytic principles or geometrical necessity.[83] In Kant's reading, Spinoza's concept of substance conflates inherence (between substance and predicates) and causality (between causes and effects); consequently, because everything is in God (i.e. the doctrine of necessity according to which everything follows the essence of God/Nature), such as the predicate in substance, there is, therefore, no place for causality,[84] especially a non-linear causality captured by reflective judgement, which is needed to account for teleology.[85] As a logical consequence, there is no space for contingency, autonomy and moral law in Spinoza's fatalism where God is lifeless. After his critique of Spinoza's fatalism, Kant reaffirms that

> For the concept of a natural end is altogether unprovable by reason in respect of its objective reality, which means that it is not constitutive for determining judgement, but merely regulative for reflective judgement.[86]

---

[80] Kant, *Critique of Judgment*, §73, 222; Ak. 5:394.

[81] Kant, *Critique of Judgment*, §73, 221; Ak. 5:393, 'aber zugleich die Zufälligkeit derselben, ohne die keine Zweckeinheit gedacht werden kann, entreißt, und mit ihr alles Absichtliche, so wie dem Urgrunde der Naturdinge allen Verstand, wegnimmt'; Zammito in *The Genesis of Kant's Critique of Judgment*, 251, summarizes Kant's charges against Spinoza, namely, Spinoza denied God 1) intelligence; 2) purposiveness; 3) freedom and 4) causality. This results in a lifeless God.

[82] For a more elaborated explanation, see Henry E. Allison, 'Kant's Critique of Spinoza', in *The Philosophy of Baruch Spinoza*, ed. Richard Kennington (Washington, DC: Catholic University of America Press, 1980), 199–277.

[83] This is also Leibniz's refusal of Spinozism, which, according to him, restricts causes to geometrical necessity and consequently denies the existence of final causes, see Gottfried Wilhelm Leibniz, *Philosophical Papers and Letters*, ed. Leroy E. Loemker (Dordrecht: D. Reidel, 1969), 478.

[84] Kant, *Critique of Judgment*, §73, 221; Ak. 5:393, 'Spinoza, as the representative of the other class, seeks to release us from any inquiry into the ground of the possibility of ends of nature, and to deprive this idea of all reality, by refusing to allow that such ends are to be regarded as products at all. They are, rather, accidents inhering in an original being. This being, he says, is the substrate of the natural things, and, as such, he does not ascribe to it causality in respect of them, but simply subsistence'.

[85] As Schelling points out in the freedom essay that the denial of freedom in Spinoza's system is not because of pantheism, but fatalism, that is to say, mechanism, see Schelling, *Philosophical Investigations into the Essence of Human Freedom*, 17. Pantheism is a principle of the formation of a system, aiming to comprehend beings in their totality, that is, *hei kai pan*; the mechanists might claim that mechanism searching for the 'all and one', but they cannot claim that pantheism is mechanism. It is beyond us here to retell the debate between Schelling and Jacobi regarding pantheism (1811–1812), for the genesis of the Schellingian system, see Hui, *Recursivity and Contingency*, Chapter 1.

[86] Kant, *Critique of Judgment*, §74, 224; Ak. 5:396.

We might want to transpose the question concerning the purposiveness of nature to the purposiveness of technology. We can determine the use of a machine according to its functionality, but it doesn't yet touch upon those metaphysical-theological and moral-practical questions, which belong to a higher purposiveness. In other words, we tend to use machines according to linear causality; for example, how they are used to reduce labour hours or improve efficiency, but we rarely use machines reflectively. Nonetheless, they can be found in certain experiences – such as amateurs learning a musical instrument or painting – where passion, rather than professional obligation, is the driving force. The purposiveness of machines is not a question of objectivity since, like the purposiveness of nature, it cannot be objectively formulated and demonstrated; thus, the purposiveness of machines could only be thought of as a projection in search of a purposiveness; something that is highly relevant to our discussion concerning the moral-practical end of machines.

When machines are thought of as a mere means to an end, as is the case in capitalism, then we expect an end which is merely associated with the accumulation of capital, which has its essence in calculability. Division of labour and automatized production are two obvious examples of why machines have been used, because they increase efficiency and reduce costs. The moral-practical end is reduced to a utilitarian end, and machines are, again, treated as a means to an end. Utopias belong to such a moral-practical end, not because they are not realizable but because they negate the means to an end by treating every being as an end in itself. The negation of the mode of thinking based on the means to an end doesn't mean that machines should be devoid of function or that all machines should become playful artworks, but rather, the use of the machine points to an end that is superior to the end it is assigned to. Considering the use of machines in factories, both Karl Marx[87] and William Morris[88] quoted John Stuart Mill's saying, 'It is questionable if all the mechanical inventions yet made have lightened the day's toil of any human being', to argue that machines, which were supposed to lighten the labour of human beings in fact only extend the length of working hours and intensify the labour process. One may argue that the true purpose of machines lies in the creation of true wealth, which Marx calls 'disposable time'.[89] It is also what Aristotle calls the end of the *polis* in *Magna*

---

[87] Karl Marx, *Capital Vol. 1*, trans. Ben Fowkes (London: Penguin Books, 1990), Chapter 15 'Machinery and Large-Scale Industry', 492.
[88] William Morris, *The Collected Works of William Morris* (Cambridge: Cambridge University Press, 2012), 'Art under Plutocracy [1883]', 180.
[89] Marx quoted C. W. Dilke's *The Source and Remedy of the National Difficulties* (1821), 'Wealth is disposable time and nothing more', see Karl Marx, *Grundrisse*, trans. Martin Nicolaus (New York:

Moralia,[90] namely, *scholê* or *otium* in Latin, which is absent as a moral demand in capitalism. *Otium* is often translated as leisure in so far it is opposed to busi-ness (*negotium*), but here we understand it closer to Marx's disposable time than the off-work time spent on entertainments, such as being addicted to video games. 'Disposable time' for Marx is neither a time that could be subordinated to the production of profit, nor is it limited to contemplation opposed to praxis as it was in ancient philosophy,[91] instead it aims at the production of knowledge and the advancement of science, both of which may not have an immediate use of exchange value, but they will contribute to a more profound progress.

By the same token, the exploitation of natural resources and the exhaustion of the planet is an ignorance of the purposiveness of nature since it reduces nature to a utilitarian end. An enterprise which excessively deforests to accumulate capital, while at the same time donating money to the poor affected by the deforestation to brand itself as an ethical enterprise, is within the calculation of means and ends, and it cannot whitewash itself from the guilt of hypocrisy. It can be true that the enterprise is happy about earning more money (as well as the benefits it obtains through its donation), and the poor are happy about receiving an unexpected donation; this doesn't exclude it from being unethical. This is why utilitarianism is not an answer to ethics, and Kant's morality helps us to understand the complexity of it. A 'universal happiness' [*allgemeine Glückseligkeit*], a term that Kant uses to conclude the 'Architectonic of Pure Reason', thought from the perspective of moral judgement should be analogous to the purposiveness of nature thought from the perspective of teleological judgement. Therefore, Kant's highest Good is where virtue (empirically unconditioned, satisfaction by pursuing a universal principle) and happiness (empirically conditioned,

---

Vintage Books, 1973), 397; a couple of pages later (401), Marx elaborates on the use of 'disposable time', 'In relation to the whole of society, the creation of *disposable time* is then also creation of time for the production of science, art etc'.

[90] Aristotle, *Magna Moralia*, trans. W.D. Ross (Oxford: Clarendon Press, 1915), 1198b, 'Does [practical reason] rule over all the faculties in the soul, which [indeed] is thought to be the case – though here there is doubt – or does it not? Because it does not seem to rule over the higher things; for instance, it does not rule over wisdom. But, it is claimed that practical reason cares for all [the faculties] and is sovereign [over the soul] with its commands. But perhaps this occurs precisely as it does in a household with the steward. Because he has authority over everything [in that] he manages everything. But he does not rule over everything, instead he prepares *scholê* for the master, so that the master may not be prevented from doing good and appropriate things on account of distractions having to do with daily necessities. Thus, in the same manner, practical reason is, in a sense, like a steward to wisdom and it prepares *scholê* for wisdom and provides it with the capability to perform its function by controlling the passions and keeping them in disciplined order'. The above quote adopts the modification of Kostas Kalimtzis, *An Inquiry into the Philosophical Concept of Scholê: Leisure as a Political End* (London: Bloomsbury, 2017), 72–3.

[91] In Aristotle's quest for the best regime of the polis, the highest end of both the individual and the city is contemplation, see Leo Strauss, *The City and Man* (Chicago, IL: Chicago University Press, 1964), 49; see also Hannah Arendt, *The Human Condition* (Chicago, IL: Chicago University Press, 1998).

satisfaction by meeting a particular need) coincide. Unlike Aristotelian ethics, which sees happiness, or human flourishing [*Eudaimonia*], as the implication of virtue, Kant distinguishes virtue from happiness. On the one hand, one can be virtuous without being happy; for example, someone who is virtuous could be abused by his neighbours who are envious of him and ends up suffering. On the other hand, one can be happy without being virtuous because, quite simply, you can use others as a means to obtain material goods and comfort. There is no necessary causality between virtue and happiness; on the contrary, as stated earlier, they might be in conflict with each other; for example, a virtuous man might be abused as a means by others, and therefore, he might lose his wealth or damage his reputation. Only when every moral agent/algorithm is operating according to the categorical imperative by recursively testing if the decision will be universal, is it possible to conceive the highest Good; otherwise, virtue and happiness don't necessarily align.[92] The highest Good stands at the end of human history, and for this reason, the realization of humanity belongs also to the end of nature, as it is pointed out by Kojève:

> It is that, by definition, a rational [*raisonnable*] life cannot be universally recognized before the end of history, for the simple reason that before this end the human World is not rational [*raisonnable*] itself (otherwise it would not change and would be the last, contrary to the supposition).[93]

Even though the highest Good is of infinite distance from us and we don't stop encountering irrationality, one can still make progress – and by progress Kant means moral progress. Machines should be directed to a different purpose which is not in accordance with being the means to an end; this means that there is a different purpose which is higher than the utilitarian one; that is to say, this purpose transcends the design principle of the machine, which is motivated by certain needs (efficiency, speed, scale, etc.) and must follow the laws of physics. This means all the effort to produce a moral artificial intelligence able to make moral decisions results from a transcendental illusion since such a decision cannot be clearly defined, nor can it be reduced to mathematics. The utilitarian purposiveness is contained in a higher purpose, which reconnects the machine to the teleology of nature. Kant had no access to thermodynamics and, therefore,

---

[92] In this sense, we can understand why in the third *Critique* Kant has to assume a communal effort in relation to the highest Good, as we can read, 'This consists in the union of the greatest welfare of the rational beings in the world with the supreme condition of their good, or, in other words, by the union of universal happiness with the strictest morality', see Kant, *Critique of Judgment*, §88, 282; Ak. 5:453).

[93] Kojève, *Kant*, 37.

to the concept of entropy. He lived in the epoch of Newtonian physics and the end of his life overlapped with the beginning of the first industrial revolution. The purposiveness of nature is a critique of Newtonian physics, that is, it is neither possible to explain the generation of a blade of grass with mechanical causes, nor could we explain it in terms of use, for example, as food for animals or shelter for insects. Therefore, between the starry heavens and the moral laws, one finds an analogy that connects the cosmos and the human, as well as the end of nature and the end of the human being. Thermodynamics not only breaks the simple mechanism and organism opposition, as Norbert Wiener has shown, but also intrudes into the analogy by turning the natural end into a dead end. The universe is moving towards its own degradation. Humans, as understood as that species which has been trying to resist entropic becoming, invented tools and changed the environment in order to restore and rebuild order; but at a certain moment, when civilization is weakened to the stage that it cannot afford such labour, its degradation will speed up. The old Kant, who suffered from dementia, in his draft of the *Opus Postumum* mixed up repetitive definitions of transcendental philosophy and system with lines of mundane reminders that discussed Marzipan, Göttingen sausages, Hamburg smoked meat, homemade English mustard, Laibkuchen, Pfefferkuchen, parsnips with mutton [*Schöpsenfleisch*], codfish, herring and potatos, etc.[94] The cosmic pessimism or even cosmic nihilism underlined by the second law of thermodynamics concerning the dissipation of energy and the becoming disorder of the cosmos is in great contrast to the natural end analogical to the moral end. On this point, Kant's teleology could be complemented by that of Simondon, especially when the author proposes to use machines to fight against the entropic becoming of the cosmos:

> The machine, as an element of the technical ensemble, becomes that which increases the quantity of information, increases negentropy, and opposes the degradation of energy: the machine, being a work of organization and information, is, like life itself and together with life, that which is opposed to disorder, to the levelling of all things tending to deprive the universe of the power of change. The machine is that through which man fights against the death of the universe; it slows down the degradation of energy, as life does, and becomes a stabilizer of the world.[95]

---

[94] The list is not exahusted here, see Immanuel Kant, *Der alte Kant: Hasse's Schrift – Letzte Äußerungen Kants*, ed. Artur Buchenau and Gerhard Lehmann (Berlin: De Gruyter, 1925)
[95] Gilbert Simondon, *On the Mode of Existence of Technical Objects*, trans. Cecile Malaspina and John Rogove (Minneapolis, MN: Univocal, 2017), 21.

This act might seem as futile as Don Quixote fighting windmills given that the second law of thermodynamics cannot be defied. However, thermodynamics remains a subject of physics; therefore, it cannot account for realms beyond that of phenomena and answer about the meaning of existence and morality. Human beings, driven by ends other than laws of physics, are like Maxwell's demons, through their prosthetic tools, trying to reverse the second law of thermodynamics. The end of the machine has to be both utilitarian and moral-practical in the sense that it serves a utilitarian purpose, while at the same time, it has another end, which is beyond the utilitarian purpose without detaching from it; this higher end cannot be standardized or normalized, but it has the function to guide us in arriving at a universal happiness, as Kant would say (even though it remains an idea of reason). The development of the machine and the opposition between it and nature, thus conceived in the eighteenth century, has been surpassed, and now, in order to think about universal happiness, the question of the machine becomes central. However, the task is not to prove if a machine is capable of being moral or not, but rather to develop an organology of morality.[96]

---

[96] An organology of morality could be seen as a response to the genealogy of morality by bringing Kant back to confront Nietzsche's unsatisfactory treatment of Kantian philosophy, which is overshadowed by Schopenhauer's interpretation. Organology, as a study of the relation between the body and its artificial organs, was credited to Henri Bergson by Georges Canguilhem in his 1947 article 'Machine and Organism', where he considers Bergson's *Creative Evolution* (1907) a foundational text on organology. Organology was further developed in the work of Simondon and Bernard Stiegler among others, with references to the work of the paleontologist André Leroi-Gourhan, to develop a historical-critical understanding of human-machine relations, especially since the industrial revolution of the eighteenth century. For a more detailed account, see Hui, *Recursivity and Contingency*, Chapter 4 'The Organizing Inorganic' and Hui, *Machine and Sovereignty*, Chapter 6 'An Organology of Wars'.

3

Peace machine

Does an algorithm of perpetual peace exist?

During the G20 Religion Forum 2022, the advisor of Pope Francis on Artificial Intelligence, Paolo Benanti, raised a question regarding the challenge of AI to peace, namely, 'do we really want AI to undermine the foundations of peace and human dignity?' The question itself already implies the negative effects of AI on peace and human dignity. What is left to answer is how to mitigate this negative tendency, especially in view of the rapid weaponization of AI. Even though automatization has been a fundamental part of the military history of the twentieth century, the direct use of AI in handling communication, decision-making and medical care has only become popular in the recent decade. Even though it has been half a century since figures such as Joseph Weizenbaum have warned that one shouldn't delegate all tasks to machines, because some are appropriate, for example inventing an automatic pilot, which is technically possible and operationally optimizable, while some are inappropriate because humans cannot be reduced to information processor,[1] it is still a popular belief (or myth) that machines could ultimately replace any task performed by humans once the so-called artificial general intelligence (AGI) is soon realized. Given the impression one has from transhumanists and computationalists, one could logically expect that in the future warfare and combat will be delegated to machines and mass destruction could take place without human deliberation due to the fact that machines are apathetic when executing kills; therefore, it also reduces mistakes caused by human sympathy.[2] In view of these threats,

---

[1] Joseph Weizenbaum, *Computer Power and Human Reason: From Judgment to Calculation* (New York: Freeman, 1976), 207.
[2] A recent report by the Guardian revealed that during the recent war in Gaza, the Israeli military has used the AI system 'Lavender' to identify 37,000 Hamas targets. According to the journalist, the soldier who uses the system admitted that he/she 'had zero added-value as a human, apart from being a stamp of approval'. See *The Guardian*, '"The Machine Did it Coldly": Israel Used AI to Identify 37,000 Hamas Targets', https://www.theguardian.com/world/2024/apr/03/israel-gaza-ai-database-hamas-airstrikes.

Benanti summarizes the church's proposal in three main points, which more or less represent the 'Rome Call for AI Ethics' initiated by the Vatican and jointly written by IBM, Microsoft, Cisco Systems, the UN's Food and Agriculture Organization, as well as the Italian government:

- Peace among us, by developing a shared language based upon timeless values;
- Peace with machines, avoiding a radical conflict between *homo sapiens* and this newborn *machina sapiens*; and
- Peace with the immense diversity of living species that dwell upon this Earth, by developing and employing innovative technologies that respect the environment in which we live and which we share with so many other life forms.[3]

All these points are sound and undeniable; human-human, human-machine, human-non-human relations are all highly politically correct research subjects prevalent in the humanities today. If we were to ask ChatGPT to outline principles for global peace, it might well give us similar answers to those outlined above, if not more complex. One expects more from the wisdom of the Pope beyond this mostly empty rhetoric. Nevertheless, it shows that decades after the work of Pierre Teilhard de Chardin— the scientist and theologian who has kind of anticipated the arrival of the internet and the so-called technological signularity[4]— the Vatican is conscious of the role of technology in the Catholic religion and that of humanity. Between the Vatican having awoken to the challenge of AI development (or the *machina sapiens*) and the popular discourse on the transition from *homo sapiens* to *homo deus*, religion and theology cannot avoid a direct confrontation with the question of technology. Technology, especially artificial intelligence, has become a crucial area that any project for peace in the twenty-first century has to address. For those, especially politicians, who wish that the world order will still be maintained by human beings (who, as it is said, now appear vulnerable in front of AI), regulations on AI have to be

---

[3] Rev. Paolo Benanti, 'Algorethics: The Timeless Values of Religion and Their Irreplaceable Contribution to the Humane and Peaceful Development of Artificial Intelligence (2022)', https://www.paolobenanti.com/post/algorethics-g20.

[4] Yuk Hui, *Machine and Sovereignty: For a Planetary Thinking* (Minneapolis, MN: University of Minnesota Press, 2024), 108-13.

imposed and must be constantly updated. To summarize, the argument of the Vatican is based on the following two premises:

1) Machines are becoming intelligent; they are becoming *machina sapiens*, therefore, a peace treaty between man and machine must be sought. We tried to differentiate humans and machines in Chapter 1, where intelligence is often either consciously or unconsciously equated with organicity.
2) Our relations to the environment and to the Other, including humans and non-humans, are mediated by machines which are now acquiring 'intelligence'. AI is not used in the same way as mechanical tools were once used, such as a hammer or a simple automaton, since it is delegated to make decisions based on sensed data and algorithms, something that has become obvious on platforms ranging from consumer goods to military commands.

Considering that machines are becoming organic, could we not imagine a system that effectively coordinates all international (as well as domestic) affairs in an 'organic' way to coordinate both supply and demand, and to balance the power and vulnerability of the states? One could even imagine the planet as a supercomputer which imitates the behaviour of a superorganism. This idea, reminiscent of the old metaphysical precept of 'oneness', resonates with those 'planetary' projects starting with 'oneness a priori', such as the recent revival of the Chinese *tianxia* (all under the heaven). But much more seductive than *tianxia*, because it is a materialist project, which proposes digitalization on a planetary scale as a candidate for the future governance of the earth. The superorganism could be composed of many organisms, similar to that of 'sympoiesis'; each organism could be an institution, a city or a state, and could be analysed in multiple layers like a 'stack', with each layer specializing in particular functions. Take digital farming as an example, modern farmers use various sensors, for example, air temperature and humidity sensors, soil moisture sensors, illumination sensors, and so on to control and automatize their greenhouses all to radically increase productivity by excluding all unfavourable factors. Each greenhouse could be coordinated so that there is no excessive supply and demand; all could be well calibrated to reduce unnecessary fluctuations. A superintelligence (or what is called an AGI, Artificial General Intelligence) – a *machina machinarum* – could be one such possibility that might transcend the differences between nation states; and it could well point to a form of planetary governance enabled by an array of sensors and artificial intelligence.

§7. Conflict of the universals

Sensors and algorithms, as some authors argue, might allow us to achieve peace. Thus, we can read white papers such as 'AI for Peace' or 'AI for Conflict Predictions', which argue that AI could allow us to predict conflicts within/between territories, reduce discrimination based on gender and race, and enforce the rights of individuals, and so on. Recently, a project from the Alan Turing Institute claims that it could use AI to predict conflict one year in advance: 'If the peacekeepers of the world, such as the United Nations, had a reliable way of predicting where conflict was likely to break out in any given city or region 12 months in advance, and deploy peacekeeping resources with pre-emptive precision, the savings in human lives and financial resources would be significant'.[5] A further improvement might be the ability to predict conflicts much earlier, such as five years or ten years in advance, so that all parties can work on their resolutions more efficiently. In the meanwhile, we have heard about some contradistinctive statements on how AI has been used to incite military aggression, identify suspects according to racial and sexual features, impose surveillance on individuals and so on. These kinds of seemingly contradictory arguments are trivial since in so far as technology is pharmacological in the sense that it is both good and bad, it is always possible to find its positive and negative uses. In other words, debating whether AI is bad or good is a modern farce. Stepping back, even if we start from a negative critique of AI by showing that the current facial recognition algorithm congeals racial bias due to the lack of data of black people or other minorities, or that ChatGPT is trained on data that biases a Western view with a 'pro-environmental, left-libertarian orientation',[6] does it mean that one should be satisfied if the facial recognition software has collected enough data to correctly identify every individual or if there would be a machine containing all world views? Paradoxically, on the one hand, these criticisms of AI often justify the development of a stronger, more powerful AI—one capable of concealing its biases more subtly; on the other hand, and even more paradoxically, such critiques of AI's inhuman limitations mask an anthropocentrism that they themselves claim to transcend.

By doing so, we become trapped in a technical argument regarding the completeness of a dataset, whether that be for facial recognition or for conflict prediction. Imagine AI predicted that there was a 55 per cent chance that Russia

---

[5] https://www.turing.ac.uk/about-us/impact/predicting-conflict-year-advance.
[6] These are said to be the findings of researchers at the Technical University of Munich and the University of Hamburg, see https://www.verdict.co.uk/peacebuilding-ai-conflict-resolution/.

was going to invade Ukraine; what could have been done otherwise? A traditional intelligence department, such as the American CIA or the German BND, might have already done a better job than AI, but the war still took place and continued with unexpected developments. Predicting and mitigating conflicts doesn't necessarily mean that peace is achievable since it could also mean an increase in pre-emptive wars, such as those we have been witnessing in the past decade; for example, the pre-emptive wars against terrorism and weapon of mass destruction (WMD) by the United States and the pre-emptive war against the perceived national threat of Ukraine and NATO by Russia. Yet some might want to defend a planetary AI by saying that if we start from the principle of oneness, then these conflicts could be internally resolved and coordinated by algorithms to optimize the gain of each party, according to the available data, albeit its incompleteness. A planetary governance or a 'world state' could be achieved electronically by integrating different states: imagine each state being represented by a supercomputer or a set of supercomputers, with supercomputers communicating with each other in order to arrive at a win-win consensus for all and to combat international crime. Given such a 'planetary computation', it might be possible to develop efficient protocols to mediate between the machines or 'rational agents'; would it not be possible in the end to achieve perpetual peace? The current technological development might well offer us a good occasion to grasp the planet both *metaphysically* and *physically* as a *whole*; in other words, it is the completion of metaphysics, the culmination of modernity.

This oneness includes various dimensions: geological, geographical, geopolitical, geobiological, geochemical and geophilosophical; it also promises effective predictions so that safe actions could be carried out to address risks, whether through geoengineering[7] or even the mitigation of warfare. The one is the universal; otherwise, it would be multiple.[8] If this is the case, then we immediately encounter an epistemological problem, which we also mentioned in the previous chapter. How are norms derived for such protocols, and whose norm should one follow? This might remind us of the classical postcolonial critique, namely whose universal are we talking about? Isn't the universal merely the norm of the winners who pronounce it, and not necessarily that of those who are asked or made to follow it? Such as during the time of the

---

[7] Notably, the EU project Destination Earth (https://destination-earth.eu/), which simulates the earth system and aims to 'provide reliable and actionable scenario predictions'.
[8] Recall that in Plato's *Parmenides*, Parmenides asked the young Aristotle 'if the one exists, the one cannot be many, can it?' Aristotle answers 'No, of course not'. (137c) On the question of the universal, we cannot escape this old Parmenidean paradox: the One being both One (137c–137d) and Many (142b–155e).

European Enlightenment, Europe became the universal and European norms were propagated throughout the globe. Given the history of colonization and modernization, it is certainly legitimate to question if what is pronounced as universal is not, in fact, suspect of being somewhat hypocritical. Carl Schmitt had something similar in mind when he approached the League of Nations and paraphrased Proudhon by saying 'whoever invokes humanity wants to cheat'.[9]

What could be called universal? Besides the technical issues that would be necessary to realize such a grand computational infrastructure, we have to answer the ontological problem, which might, indeed, render all technical efforts meaningless. The universal is often opposed to the particular, and universalism to relativism; but does this mean that the universal signifies something shared in common? We can say that global warming is a *common* problem, but we cannot say it is a *universal* one; it might well be a big problem for those humans who have lived in stable climates for centuries, but is it also valid for all other living beings or even for the future humans to come? Besides learning from statistics, which can never reflect all the real causes since a phenomenon like global warming might well have complex hidden causes, we might never know the answer to this question. We can at most agree that global warming constitutes a problem for *most* of the human inhabitants on the earth; it is an *empirical fact* which we cannot easily deny. And, in the same fashion, one can turn to anything that is publicly announced as universal and question its universal validity, for example, the 'Universal Declaration of Human Right.' Indeed, we shouldn't forget that the Universal Declaration of Human Rights was only established in 1948, and that since this very date, which is to say after Israel's occupation of their land, the Palestinians have been continually refused the right to a state. Not until 2024, that is to say almost eighty years later, have some countries such as Spain and South Africa started to recognize Palestine as a state. Today, it has become almost obvious, as many theorists do, to criticize that the universal is nothing but historically constructed and that behind any such claim lies the fullness of hypocrisy. Even in the domain of science, where systems of knowledge are grounded in universality, we are still waiting for a grand universal theory which is capable of unifying the theory of relativity and quantum mechanics. Does this mean that we should completely abandon the concept of the universal, which originally means *for and belongs to all*?

---

[9] Carl Schmitt, *The Concept of the Political*, trans. George Schwab (Chicago, IL: The University of Chicago Press, 1996), 54.

This reminds us of the scholastic debate between realism and nominalism, in which the latter rejects any universal category (i.e. species and genus) as being real (i.e. being a thing) and insists that only the particular is real: you can see this and that apple, but you don't see the apple. The rejection of the universal in the political realm gives rise to a political nominalism or a cultural relativism. The turn to cultural relativism has been the central subject of postcolonialism, and it continues in various domains, even philosophy – considering the trend of adding a nationality to philosophy today: German philosophy, French philosophy, Indian philosophy, Chinese philosophy, Japanese philosophy and so on. Should relativism be the answer to the crisis of our epoch? However, it might be too lazy, if not too cynical, to give up any attempt to conceive a protocol which can bring us perpetual peace, or at least to improve the well-being of the planet and to avoid large-scale disasters brought about by the foolishness of humans. To problematize it with a concrete example: once one counters European universalism with cultural relativism and provincializes the former, then should one also respect countries which repress women precisely because this has been part of their tradition? If state oppressions could be simply justified as internal affairs, then history will stagnate, and human beings will be returned to a compromised barbarianism – compromised in the sense that reason has to pretend that nothing irrational happens: 'Everything's gonna be alright'. A just war or a regular war is a potential answer to this stagnation.[10] This is why we should return to Kant, the great philosopher of the universal, in order to rediscover the universal but also the possibility of a peace machine. Kant didn't mediate between the cosmos and the human via the machine; instead, human subjectivity is said to be the ground of cognition, desire and feeling. One could reproach Kant for being anthropocentric or for being, as the contemporary philosopher Quentin Meillassoux calls him, a correlationist and a humanist;[11] according to this accusation, Kantian epistemology reduces the world of objects to the subjective experience of objects. However, Kant is much more sophisticated than the strawman Meillassoux has presented. First of all, Kant understands that the whole system of knowledge changes when the understanding shifts from the human to another living being;[12] second, Kant also saw the significance of rational ideas such as the immortal Soul, God, Freedom

---

[10] This is the proposal of Hegel in *Outlines of the Philosophy of Right*, where he claims that each state should be viewed as individual and therefore shouldn't interfere in each other's internal affairs; however, when mutual recognition is not reached, war is inevitable; see Hegel, *Outlines of the Philosophy of Right*, trans. T. M. Knox (Oxford: Oxford University Press, 2008), §259.

[11] Quentin Meillassoux, *After Finitude: An Essay on the Necessity of Contingency*, trans. Ray Brassier (London: Continuum, 2008).

[12] Kant, 'On a Pure Mysticism in Religion (Appendix)', in *Conflict of the Faculties*, trans. Mary J. Gregor (New York: Abaris Books, 1979), 129; *Ak.* 7:70, 'given another understanding, another world would

and the thing-in-itself, which the human subject cannot have sufficient knowledge of and which could never be objects of experience, but which one nonetheless has to postulate in order to render a moral life coherent. It is true though that in Kant, machines are either used as a proxy to distinguish the specificity and complexity of human existence, or they are already subsumed to his organicism, namely, the technical presupposes the organic, as Georges Canguilhem puts it.[13] It is a vague organology we can interpret in Kant – and by organology, we mean the understanding of technical tools as artificial organs and the study of the integration of such organs into the human body and community. It is vague since it was never spelt out explicitly in Kant's texts, though one could speculate that it was already unintentionally presupposed, like water to fish and air to mammals. Indeed, it is possible to trace the primacy of an organic epistemology in the conceptualization of politics since the eighteenth century, as *Machine and Sovereignty* aimed to deliver by analysing Hegel's justification of the organic state as the only political form in which freedom is possible.[14] And as we have been trying to show here, and did more systematically in *Recursivity and Contingency*, that Kant was probably the first philosopher to develop a systematic account of organicity; the organismic epistemology is fundamental to almost all aspects of his critical philosophy, including politics. It is, therefore, still worth returning to Kant to look at how specifically in the late Kant, in his treatise on perpetual peace, machines are subsumed to the organic structure and the reflective operation.

In the late Kant (1795–8), what we want to discover is the *peace machine*; more specifically, we want to show that Kant's *Perpetual Peace: A Philosophical Sketch* (1795)[15] could be read as such an attempt to conceive of an algorithm that aims at perpetual peace without presupposing a universal norm. In other words, Kant didn't start by imposing a universal rule or a universal norm, for example, a pre-established harmony for all the states; instead, Kant recognizes the particularity of each player (each of them is free, independent and equal)

---

also exist, as the example of insanity makes clear'.
[13] Georges Canguilhem, *Knowledge of Life*, trans. Stefanos Geroulanos and Daniela Ginsburg (New York: Fordham University Press, 2008), 92–3, where Canguilhem cited Paul Krannhals's *Der Weltsinn der Technik* and commented that Krannhals 'sees in it, rightly, it would seem, a recognition of the fact that every technique essentially and positively *includes a vital originality irreducible to rationalization*'. (Italics are mine)
[14] Hui, *Machine and Sovereignty*, Chapter 2.
[15] The pamphlet was written after two significant events: first, Prussia's withdrawal from the war with France in 1795, witnessed by the Treaty of Basel, and second, Prussia's participation in the third and final partition of Poland (the first two were in 1772 and 1793). Kant's pamphlet is courageous, with an ironic and sometimes melancholic tone; it was also carefully articulated in order not to be targeted by the state.

as well as the difficulty of sociability[16] and injects into the algorithm of peace a genetic dynamic. Kant's perpetual peace implies two different concepts of the universal corresponding to regulative and constitutive principles. As we consistently stated in the previous chapters, constitutive principles define the structure of the object of experience and could be applied to all possible experiences, just as the understanding does to sense data; regulative principles, conversely, heuristically guide our reasoning and inquiry without defining the content of experience, such as the ideas of reason do. Determinative judgements follow constitutive principles, starting with a given universal and apply them to every particular; reflective judgements follow regulative principles, starting with the particular and reflectively search for the universal, which is neither given a priori nor guaranteed a posteriori. This is clearly indicated in the antinomy of judgement in the third *Critique*, which we propose to interpret as a testimony on the two universals. The original formulation that Kant gives us is quoted below:

> Thesis: All production of material things and their forms must be judged as possible on mere mechanical laws.
>
> Antithesis: Some products of material nature cannot be judged as possible on mere mechanical laws (that is, for judging them quite a different law of causality is required, namely, that of final causes).[17]

Mechanical laws, here, mean the universal laws of physics (and mathematics) that govern the body's movement; for example, Newton's classical mechanics. This form of causality is linear, meaning one effect can be traced to one cause, and the causal chain continues until the first cause can be identified. In mechanism, the universal is already given in the form of the laws of physics. Teleology concerns final causes and does not share the same kind of causality as mechanical laws; its causality is non-linear (or recursive, as I elaborated in *Recursivity and Contingency*); the universal is not yet given, and one needs a heuristic to search for it. Kant didn't resolve the antinomy by simply rejecting mechanism nor by simply endorsing teleology; instead, Kant maintained the necessity of both mechanism and teleology. In §79 of the Appendix to the *Critique of Judgment*, Kant affirms again that 'this science [natural science] requires determining, and

---

[16] As Arendt points out, the question of sociability and the question of the purposiveness of existence occupied the late Kant, see Hannah Arendt, *Lectures on Kant's Political Philosophy* (Chicago, IL: The University of Chicago Press, 1982), 10–12. We would like to emphasize that sociability doesn't mean harmony or community, but rather conflicts, which, for Kant, the Christian stoic, are necessary to defer the deterioration of the physical body and reason.

[17] Immanuel Kant, *Critique of Judgment*, trans. James Creed Meredith and Nicholas Walker (Oxford: Oxford University Press, 2007), §70, 214–5; Ak. 5:387–8.

not merely reflective, principles for the purpose of assigning objective grounds of natural effects'.[18] Kant's resolution is that the semblance of the two theses originates from the confusion of the reflective judgement with determinative judgement. In other words, the universal claimed to be given a priori shouldn't be conflated with the universal, which is not yet given but whose existence is necessary:

> All semblance of an antinomy between the maxims of the strictly physical, or mechanical, mode of explanation and the teleological, or technical, rests, therefore, on our confusing a principle of reflective with one of determining judgement. The *autonomy* of the former, which is valid merely subjectively for the use of our reason in respect of particular empirical laws, is mistaken for the *heteronomy* of the second, which has to conform to the laws, either universal or particular, given by the understanding.[19]

Kant wants to say that the antinomy comes from a confused misuse of determinative and reflective judgement. Without differentiating the two and their respective uses, one will be thrown again and again into confusion. Therefore, we might say that the postcolonial critique of the universal belongs to the critique of the first universal, that is to say, one that follows a constitutive principle like mechanical laws. Modernization could be seen as the application of constitutive principles, or the exercise of an old metaphysics, by placing the one prior to the many and serving as the latter's source. When we look at the textbooks on science and technology studied in modern schools, the knowledge in these textbooks claims its validity and universality partly due to the domination and colonization of the West; a *thorough* postcolonial critique – were it possible at all – would have to reject both science and technology as well as their applications because they have both been conceived as universal. This would nevertheless be an illusion caused by an overdose of nostalgia. Another way to confront it is to look into the second universal, since without it we will not be able to conceive any betterment of human history, nor would we be able to determine any progress of planetary history. This second universal appears immediately to be a negative concept. By negative concept here we mean a universality with negativity, namely, to claim something universal we should assume that the true universal is *not yet* there. A conundrum emerges, for if the universal is negative in itself, what might be the advantage of talking about it? Because when the one is placed prior to the many, it exerts an authority over the

---

[18] Kant, *Critique of Judgment*, §79, 245; Ak. 5:416.
[19] Kant, *Critique of Judgment*, §71, 217; Ak. 5:389.

rest; why would one want to talk about a universality without authority, that is to say, one that is not yet there and that no one knows even how to obey? We could answer that the universal in so far as it is a negative concept is also an affirmative concept in the sense that one should look beyond the many in order to search for the one; however, it is not about the elimination of difference, but rather there is a completely different heuristic which allows us to transcend a simple, linear and positive universal and to rediscover a *pluralism* without conflating it with arbitrary relativism. We arrive at a paradox concerning this form of universality shared by aesthetic and teleological judgement. Kant is aware of the difficulty of claiming something as being universal without imposing a pre-established harmony at the beginning, and in contrast to that, he recognizes the unsocial sociality of the human being: 'their propensity to enter into society, which, however, is combined with a thoroughgoing resistance that constantly threatens to break up this society'.[20] In other words, the many appears as a default and the one, unlike the already given, is absent. Kant's understanding of the emergence of law and state is closer to Thomas Hobbes's discourse on the move from the state of nature to the civil state than to that of Jean-Jacques Rousseau. For Hobbes, the world begins with a state of nature which is described as a war of 'all against all' which is hypothesized according to the report of the missionaries about 'many places in America',[21] while Rousseau postulates a world of harmony of the original men, whose prototype is found among the Caribbeans,[22] prior to degradation. We know that according to Hobbes, in order to get out of the state of nature, namely, a state of chaos and the war of all against all, each individual has to surrender to the sovereign power in order to exchange it for protection. Civil law endows rights and demands obligation (to the sovereignty). The contract between the individual and the state has its foundation in natural laws, namely, a set of rational principles for self-preservation. In *The Metaphysics of Morals* (1797), Kant emphasizes the necessity of moving away from the state of nature and never returning to it to avoid the war of all against all. One could compare law/right with geometry since, as Kant says, by analogy 'the theory of right will also seek an assurance that each individual receives (with mathematical precision) what is his *due*'; but Kant immediately claims that this cannot be

---

[20] Immanuel Kant, 'Idea for a University History with Cosmopolitan Aim', in *Kant's Idea for a Universal History with a Cosmopolitan Aim: A Critical Guide*, ed. Amélie Oksenberg Rorty and James Schmidt (Cambridge: Cambridge University Press, 2009), Fourth Proposition, 13, Ak. 8:21.
[21] Thomas Hobbes, *Leviathan* (Indianapolis, IN: Hackett, 1994), Chapter 13, 77.
[22] Jean-Jacques Rousseau, *The Social Contract and the First and Second Discourses* (New Haven, CT and London: Yale University Press, 2002), 110, where he claims that the Caribbeans are 'who have as yet deviated least from the state of nature'!'

expected of ethics, since ethics 'cannot refuse to allow some room for exceptions (*latitudienem*)'.[23] Moving out of the state of nature doesn't imply that hostility and conflict will be overcome as, for example, a geometrical problem is resolved once and for all. Instead, conflict will persist and even become necessary for thinking the universal. This is best exemplified in Kant's late work, the three articles plus appendixes that he presented in *Conflict of the Faculties* (1798).

We recall that in the *Conflict of the Faculties*, Kant opposes the lower faculty to the other three higher faculties, namely, theology, law and medicine. It is important to notice that Kant calls it conflict [*Streit*] and not war; there is a *need* for a permanent conflict *without* war. It would be too simple to understand that Kant was only talking about the university alone, namely the necessary presence of a philosophical faculty, which is very much weakened or even seen to be disappearing in our time, or which is often subordinated to interdisciplinary programmes in order to become 'productive' and 'useful'. The faculty of philosophy in Kant's time includes two departments, as Kant tells us: the department of historical knowledge (including history, geography, philology and the humanities, along with all the empirical knowledge contained in the natural sciences) and a department of pure rational knowledge (pure mathematics and pure philosophy, the metaphysics of nature and of morals).[24] Kant didn't say, as many contemporaries do, that philosophy should remain 'useless' and must not become useful in any case. Instead, he sees that the function of the philosophy faculty in relation to the other three is to control [*kontrollieren*] them and to be useful [*nützlich*] to them,[25] because all faculties should primarily concern truth, which is the domain of philosophy, while usefulness to the government should be a secondary task. The philosophy faculty mentioned above is large, but Kant doesn't speak for geography or history; he speaks for 'pure philosophy', namely, the metaphysics of nature and morals.

Retrospectively, Kant's texts[26] were revolts against the edict of censorship against his work on religion issued by King Fredrich Wilhelm II as per the request of the High Ecclesiastical Councillor [*Oberkonsistorialrat*].[27] Outraged, Kant

---

[23] Kant, 'The Metaphysics of Morals', in Immanuel Kant, *Political Writings*, trans. H. B. Nisbet, ed. H. S. Reiss (Cambridge: Cambridge University Press, 1991), 135; Ak. 6:233.
[24] Kant, *Conflict of the Faculties*, 45; Ak. 7:28.
[25] Kant, *Conflict of the Faculties*, 45; Ak. 7:28.
[26] In the Preface of *Conflict of the Faculties*, we read that the idea of compiling the three articles and publishing them as an individual work came to Kant later; the first text could be seen as the most fundamental outline of the conflict; the second text discusses human progress, and the third text, which was originally Kant's letter written in 1798 replying to the physician Christoph Wilhelm Hufeland, who sent him his book *On the Art of Prolonging Human Life* in 1796.
[27] Kant told in the preface of *Conflict of the Faculties* that he received a religious edict and later an edict of censorship from King Friedrich Wilhelm II, issued on 1 October 1794, which accused Kant

defended himself, but he also assured the King that he would 'refrain altogether from discoursing publicly, in lectures or writings, on religion, whether natural or revealed'.[28] Still, Kant rebelled by reintroducing conflict to the faculties. The conflict of faculties is Kant's further development of the implications of his second critique (and inevitably also the third critique), namely the absolute faith in reason as the condition of moral progress – for Kant, true progress is moral progress, and any political revolution which doesn't lead to moral progress is not desirable. The revolt of the Königsberger is that faith in reason gives way to the magical play of the scholars from the higher faculties. The magicians of the higher faculties lure the masses to dogmas and even superstitions without recognizing the place of reason and its appropriate use. Kant expresses his critique with a sense of humour:

> the demands they make on these scholars run like this 'as for the philosophers' twaddle, I've known that all along. What I want you, as men of learning, to tell me is this: if I've been a scoundrel all my life, how can I get an eleventh-hour ticket to heaven? If I've broken the law, how can I still win my case? And even if I've used and abused my physical powers as I have pleased, how can I stay healthy and live a long time? Surely this is why you have studied – so that you would know more than someone like ourselves (you call us laymen), who can claim nothing more than sound understanding.'[29]

These demands for the good by circumscribing reason make the 'businessmen [*Geschäftsleute*]' of the three higher faculties appear like magicians, as Kant calls them. If one could go to heaven without doing too much good, and one can have more enjoyment without paying too much effort, isn't this more desirable than its opposite? This might well resonate with what is happening today with the fantasy of technological acceleration and the illusion that almost everything could be resolved through technology: human enhancement, *homo deus*, algorithmic optimization, quantified self and so on. The transhumanist proposal that lifespan, intelligence and emotion could be technologically enhanced or improved is a wholesale of modern indulgences. The dream of an AGI to resolve all human problems is another version of pursuing enjoyment without

---

of having misused his philosophy over a long period of time 'to distort and disparage many of the cardinal and basic teachings of the Holy Scriptures and of Christianity' and excepted 'better things of you, as you yourself must realize how irresponsibly you have acted against your duty as a teacher of youth and against our paternal purpose, which you know well'. Kant's work is a direct response, or more precisely a transcendental refusal, to these accusations. See also Ernst Cassirer, *Kant's Life and Thought*, trans. James Haden (New Haven, CT: Yale University Press, 1983), 380–1.

[28] Kant, *Conflict of the Faculties*, 19; Ak. 7:10.
[29] Kant, *Conflict of the Faculties*, 51; Ak. 7:31.

paying effort; it is an 'administrative nihilism' in its most naive and laziest sense. Kant wants to suggest that the domination of the businessmen will continue undermining reason if the philosophy faculty is not allowed to counteract them publicly.[30] It is because reason should be fundamental to theology, which concerns an ethical religious life; law, which concerns human progress; and medical science, which concerns having a long and healthy life. In Kant's answer to 'What is Enlightenment (1784)', we are already reminded that one should be given the freedom 'to make *public use* of one's reason in all matters' in order to address the 'entire reading public'.[31] Taking the example of religion, the Bible presents us with many miracles that cannot be explained without recourse to supernatural power. One might have to rely on the theologians to provide 'authentic' interpretations and dogmas. Which dogma is more universal than the other? Kant confronts again the problem of the universal and affirms that:

> To claim *universal validity* for a dogma (*catholicismus hierarchies*) involves a contradiction: for unconditioned universality presupposes necessity, and since this occurs only where reason itself provides sufficient grounds for the tenets of faith, no mere statute can be universally valid.[32]

Given these differences and the difficulty of any school to claim the universal, one is easily trapped in religious conflicts. Now, Kant notices that some 'false peacemakers (syncretists)' would arise and attempt to please everyone by melting down the different creeds.[33] Beyond the religious context, one could imagine a more contemporary scenario, whereby claiming that there is a planetary crisis, the public intellectuals request all the states to give up their differences and focus on resolving the common problem regarding climate change. We hear this kind of good intention a lot from UN committees as well as the mass media and think tanks; or we could also think of the possibility of a superintelligence which is able to outdo human beings in terms of all political, economic and social planning, for politics is nothing but the means to resolve the mistakes made by humans (i.e. politics belongs to a human epistemology). What does Kant think about these 'false peacemakers'? Kant says '[t]hese syncretists are even worse than sectarians, because they are basically indifferent to religion in general and take the attitude that, if the people must have dogma, one is as good as another so long as it lends itself readily to the government's aims'.[34] In other

---

[30] Kant, *Conflict of the Faculties*, 51; Ak. 7:31.
[31] Kant, 'What is Enlightenment', in *Political Writings*, 55; Ak. 8:35.
[32] Kant, *Conflict of the Faculties*, 87; Ak. 7:49.
[33] Kant, *Conflict of the Faculties*, 91; Ak. 7:51.
[34] Kant, *Conflict of the Faculties*, 91; Ak. 7:51.

words, these 'peacemakers' pretend to have dissolved all conflicts and differences and subsume all to the interest of an institution such as a government or an ideology. Kant never endorsed the need for beautiful tranquillity in a golden age since, for him, such a demand is nothing but a poet's 'empty longing [*leere Sehnsucht*]'.[35] What Kant calls poets here are the fiction-theorists of our time. Who, then, might be a true peacemaker? Kant's answer to it would be 'whereas dogma requires historical scholarship, reason alone is sufficient for religious faith'.[36]

§8. Algorithm of perpetual peace

The conflict of the faculties between philosophy and other faculties [*Fakultäten*] stands here as a prototype with which we can look into the conflict within philosophy itself, namely the conflict between critical philosophy and other philosophical schools, the conflict between speculative-theoretical reason and moral-practical reason. It also implies the conflict between the faculty [*Vermögen*] of cognition, the faculty of desire and the faculty of feeling. In 'Proclamation of the imminent conclusion of a treaty of perpetual peace in philosophy' (1796),[37] Kant started with a discourse on the *physical cause* of philosophy. Kant suggests that besides human's self-consciousness which granted them the title of rational animal and distinguishes them from other animals, there is another physical cause which he calls an itch [*Hang*] and later considers it as a drive [*Drang*]:

> there is also the itch to use this power for *trifling* [*zum Vernünfteln zu bestimmen*], and thereafter to trifle methodologically and even by concepts alone, i.e., to *philosophize*; and then also to grate polemically upon others with one's philosophy, i.e., to *dispute* [*reiben*], and since this does not readily happen without emotion, to *squabble* [*zanken*] on behalf of one's philosophy, and finally,

---

[35] Kant, 'Mutmaßlicher Anfang der Menschengeschichte', *Ak.* 8:122, 'wo eine Entziehung von allem eingebildeten Bedürfnissen, das uns die Unglück aufladet, sein soll, eine Gemeinschaft mit dem bloßen Bedarf der Natur, eine durchgängige Gleichheit der Menschen, ein ununterbrochener Friede unter ihnen, mit einem Worte der reine Genuß eines sorgenfreien, in Faulheit verdummten oder mit kindischen Spiel verträndelten Lebens'; also quoted by Hans Saner, *Kants Political Thought: Its Origin and Development* (Chicago, IL: The University of Chicago Press, 1973), 252.
[36] Kant, *Conflict of the Faculties*, 79; *Ak.* 7:45.
[37] This article was preceded by another article titled 'On a Recently Prominent Tone of Superiority in Philosophy', both published by the *Berlinische Monatsschrift* in 1796. The target of Kant's criticism was a book titled *Plato's Letters about the State Revolution of Syracuse* (1795), written by the amateur philosopher Johann Georg Schlosser (who happened to be a brother-in-law of Goethe). For the historical background, see the editorial note in Kant, *Theoretical Philosophy after 1781*, trans. Hatfield et al., ed. Henry Allison et al. (Cambridge: Cambridge University Press, 2009), 427–8.

united in masses against one another (school against school, as contending armies) to wage *open warfare [offenen Krieg]*.[38]

This itch, which underlines all conflicts in philosophy, is considered by Kant to be 'one of the beneficent and wise arrangements of Nature, whereby she seeks to protect man from the great misfortune of decaying in the living fresh'.[39] It also implies that philosophy is not a static system of knowledge which one can learn, since it demands disturbances, and therefore, one can learn only to *philosophize*.[40] One could read in this essay that what Kant has to confront here are not only the attacks from the ecclesiastical theologians but also from those philosophers who consider that his discourse on the supersensible is exactly what philosophy must get rid of.[41] Without the distinction between the sensible and the supersensible, it would be impossible for critical philosophy to elaborate on morality and freedom, because without this distinction, noumenon will be reduced to phenomenon, and the faculty of desire would collapse into mere physiological and empirical inclinations. Numbers and data are essential to understand the world, but the world is far more than number and data. In Chapter 2, we saw that Kojève believed that Kant abandoned the thing-in-itself in favour of the mode of 'as if' and thus transformed his system into a Hegelian system of knowledge. Kojève was partially correct in the sense that he saw the importance of the reflective judgement as the operation of the system; however, he failed to understand that the noumenal entities remain compatible with the mode of 'as if'. In other words, one could equally claim that the mode of 'as if' is a new invention that accommodates the unknowability of the noumenon.

The conflict between religion and philosophy could likewise be projected onto the conflict between states, for one can also find physical causes such as the 'itch' mentioned above among the states. Conflicts might evolve gradually into wars over time or mutate rapidly into wars due to the sudden trigger of contingent factors. How could peace be possible if one doesn't allude to a superintelligence governing the whole planet? Kant is sceptical of any global governing body or world sovereignty since it might easily violate the three principles of freedom, independence and equality concerning all sovereign

---

[38] Kant, 'Treaty of Perpetual Peace in Philosophy', in *Theoretical Philosophy after 1781*, 453; *Ak.* 8:414.
[39] Kant, 'Treaty of Perpetual Peace in Philosophy', 453; *Ak.* 8:414.
[40] Immanuel Kant, *Critique of Pure Reason*, trans. Werner S. Pluhar (Indianapolis, IN: Hackett, 1996), A837, B865, 'But philosophy can never be learned (except historically); rather, as far as reason is concerned, one can at most learn only *to philosophize*'. (italics are original)
[41] Schlosser harshly criticized Kant in his *Schreiben an einen jungen Mann, der die Kantische Philosophie studieren wollte* (1796), which Kant quoted as the following: 'all imitations, vistas of the super-sensible, every genius of the poetic are to have their wings clipped'. See Kant, 'Treaty of Perpetual Peace in Philosophy', 458; *Ak.* 8:420.

states. This precisely distinguishes him from Christian Wolff, who supports a supreme state or a universal commonwealth (*civitas maxima*). However, unlike Rousseau, who is sceptical of any confederation or union of all European states (i.e. a proposal from Abbé de Saint-Pierre which Rousseau considers too utopian due to the unwillingness of the individual states, but also because the scale and diversity are too large, for it to take place an undesirable violent revolution ought to take place),[42] Kant only endorses some loosely connected 'union of states' or 'league of peace' (*foedus pacificum*) which can be dissolved at any time and which doesn't form a new legal entity such as a world republic or a world state.[43] Indeed, he is even sceptical of any super-large union of states because such a union, he believes, would eventually become impossible to govern and therefore it would end up inciting war;[44] that, or it will become like China (as Kant understood), being in a stable status and not being attacked by any major enemy, but ending up being 'stripped [of] every vestige of freedom'.[45] Kant refuses both the school of just wars (Augustine, Suarez, Wolff) which legitimates wars by instrumentalizing morality and the school of regular wars (Grotius, Pufendorf, Vattel) which legitimates wars on the basis of legality,[46] and indeed he calls the latter three 'tiresome comforters' [*lauter leidige Tröster*] whose theories didn't move the states to avoid war and achieve peace as they intended to; instead, they are mobilized by the states to justify military aggressions.[47] In other words, unlike these authors who ponder upon *how to fight war justly and legally*, Kant's question is rather *how to eliminate war completely*. It is a truism to see that each state, insofar as it is free and independent, has the right to wage war for the purpose of self-preservation or retaliation. Yet it remains within the state of nature, that is to say, a non-juridical condition of society and therefore unjust.[48]

---

[42] See Jean-Jacques Rousseau, 'Abstract and Judgment of Saint-Pierre's Project for Perpetual Peace', trans. C. E. Vaughan, in *Rousseau on International Relations*, ed. Stanley Hoffmann and David P. Fidler (Oxford: Oxford University Press, 1991), 100, 'No federation could ever be established except by a revolution. That being so, which of us would dare to say whether the league of Europe is a thing more to be desired or feared? It would perhaps do more harm in a moment than it would guard against for ages'. To note that the 'Abstract' which presents and defends Saint-Pierre's plan was published in 1761, in which Rousseau proposes five articles to realize such a confederation; and the 'Judgment' was published in 1782, in which Rousseau demonstrates that its realization is *impossible*. On the contrary, Rousseau found small confederations such as the Swiss Confederation more realistic, in which the cantons remain relatively independent and respect each other.

[43] Kant, 'Die Metaphysik der Sitten', Ak. 6:351, also quoted by Ripstein, *Kant and the Law of War*, 224.

[44] Kant, *The Metaphysics of Morals*, 156, Ak. 6:350.

[45] Kant, 'Conjectural Beginning of Human History (1786)', in *Political Writings*, 231; Ak. 8:121.

[46] Kant, 'Toward Perpetual Peace', 79, Ak. 8:355; see also Ripstein, *Kant and the Law of War*, 10.

[47] Kant, 'Toward Perpetual Peace', 79, Ak. 8:355. This, however, doesn't suggest that Kant was not influenced by them, because the opposite is true; this is self-evident in Kant's writings, especially 'Toward Perpetual Peace'.

[48] Charles Covell, *Kant and the Law of Peace: A Study in the Philosophy of International Law and International Relations* (London: Palgrave Macmillan, 1998), 108.

Kant sees the avoidance of war within the possibility of moral-practical reason, as he says in the conclusion of the 'Doctrine of Right' in *The Metaphysics of Morals*:

> Now, moral-practical reason within us pronounces the following irresistible veto: *There shall be no war*, either between individual human beings in the state of nature, or between separate states, which, although internally law-governed, still live in a lawless condition in their external relationships with one another. For war is not the way in which anyone should pursue his rights.[49]

We find that the transcendental principle of perpetual peace is indeed shared by religion, philosophy and politics. Kant claims in the conclusion of the first part 'The Conflict of the Philosophy Faculty with the Theology Faculty' with the title 'Conclusion of Peace and Settlement of the Conflict of the Faculties' that 'in any conflict having to do only with pure but practical reason, no one can dispute the prerogative of the philosophy faculty to make the report'.[50] In this sense, the dogmas shouldn't be respected as the ultimate explanation of the holy scripture; instead, pure practical reason should be considered as the true resolution of the conflicts. In an Appendix to it titled 'On a Pure Mysticism in Religion', Kant confesses to the 'venerable father' about his encounter with the mystics or separatists and uses it as a counterexample to the ecclesiastics by saying that 'it was indeed difficult to recognize your teachings, at first, in their mystical terms, but after persistent probing I succeeded . . . though they take as their code not the Bible, but only the precepts of an inward Christianity dwelling in us from eternity'.[51] Kant ironically uses the mystics and the separatists to attack the businessmen of the theology faculty because, in comparison to the businessmen, the mystics and separatists are much closer to the Bible, even though in reality they were also reproached by the ecclesiastics. It is because, as we can understand, they have faith in reason; therefore, they are able to use pure practical reason appropriately to lead to a moral life – moral in the sense of the *categorical imperative*.

In the 'Treatise of Perpetual Peace in Philosophy', Kant claims that a peace treaty between the schools of philosophy could be constituted, or nearly settled, if 'the parties [were to] understand one another [*sich einander nur versteht*]'.[52] Now, we might want to suspect Kant of falling back into a kind of negotiationism,

---

[49] Kant, 'The Metaphysics of Morals', 174, Ak. 6:354.
[50] Kant, *Conflict of the Faculties*, 111; Ak. 7:61.
[51] Kant, *Conflict of the Faculties*, 137; Ak. 7:74.
[52] Kant, 'Treaty of Perpetual Peace in Philosophy', 459; Ak. 8:421.

something which is shared among some postcolonial critics who have proposed it as a renewed process that aims towards the universal.[53] In other words, recognizing and understanding each other's difference while preserving a certain form of harmony. Kant, of course, cannot entertain this relapse into empiricism or this pragmatic manoeuvre. By understanding one another, Kant means that each school of philosophy recognizes the difference between theoretical reason and practical reason and limits science to theoretical reason while expanding reason to the supersensible realm without which freedom would be impossible. Reason is the key to the resolution, but philosophers will need faith in reason; such a faith is not a superstition but rather has its source in truthfulness, in the sense that everything a philosopher says must be truthful [*wahrhaftig*],[54] 'especially in what to do with the super-sensible' as Kant emphasizes.[55] One may want to call it *sincerity*, but Kant, the 'great Chinaman of Königsberg' as Nietzsche called him,[56] might be sceptical of any pretension of sincerity precisely because it sounds too Chinese: in the next line he humorously mocks the Chinese merchants for writing over their shops in golden letters: 'No cheating here'. In the end, the peace treaty in philosophy demands a return to itself as a doctrine of wisdom, which recursively searches for truth and defends reason in a form analogous to the *categorical imperative*.

How is this possible when we take the rivalry between different states into account? Inside the state, or more precisely what he calls a *free state* in contradistinction from an absolute state, Kant tells us that one should look for a constitution, or a republicanism, which approximates the principle of rights. This constitution will be the unity of the legislative, executive and juridical powers, and under the condition that 'reason, *by a categorical imperative*, obliges us to strive for its realisation'.[57] This remark is significant, since Kant is not only proposing a framework of right which accommodates the cosmopolitan right of visitation but also a system which is at the same time moral and practical. The 'categorical imperative', the magical word, the *deus ex machina*, is behind the peace treatise inside of religion, philosophy and politics. However, the question

---

[53] Souleymane Bachir Diagne, for example, gave some sharp criticisms of a universalism of one culture; recognizing the need for the universal, he, however, arrives at a 'universality of negotiation', see Karen Van Dyck & Souleymane Bachir Diagne (7 February 2024), 'In conversation: Karen Van Dyck speaks with Souleymane Bachir Diagne: mutuality and unexpected collaboration in translation', *The Translator*, https://doi.org/ 10.1080/13556509.2023.2275806.
[54] Kant, 'Treaty of Perpetual Peace in Philosophy', 459; *Ak*. 8:421.
[55] Kant, 'Treaty of Perpetual Peace in Philosophy', 460; *Ak*. 8:422.
[56] See Friedrich Nietzsche, *Beyond Good and Evil: Prelude to a Philosophy of the Future*, trans. Judith Norman (Cambridge: Cambridge University Press, 2002), Aphorism 210.
[57] Kant, 'The Metaphysics of Morals', 143; *Ak*. 6:298.

still remains: How could we understand the 'categorical imperative' operating in international politics, if one neither aspires to a world sovereign state nor agrees upon any predefined 'universal values'?

The common interpretation of a federation of states and cosmopolitan right constrained by a moral demand doesn't seem to have sufficiently explained the mechanism at work; for we could also find similar proposals in philosophers before Kant such as Grotius, Wolff, Pufendorf and Vattle. In *Perpetual Peace*, Kant discusses in detail the international rights between states and individuals, that is, visiting rights and hospitality. In the 'Final Supplement: On the Guarantee of Perpetual Peace', we can find a concrete example of international trade, which functions almost like an algorithm and realizes the federation of states as an organism. Note that Kant has to confront not only how morality is possible but also how the pursuit of morality could facilitate perpetual peace. It is here that moral teleology and political teleology converge; thus Karl-Otto Apel could claim that 'once we rethink teleology in terms of opportunities to realize the cosmopolitan order of law and peace in history, it is also possible to reevaluate Kant's assessment of the positive means that help realize these goals'.[58] Apel rightly observes that there are three elements essential to this realization, namely, 'spirit of commerce', republican constitution and publicity 'of all the demands and the claims connected with law'.[59] These elements were equally pronounced by Kant, but we still need to elaborate on what kind of operation could guarantee the realization of such a teleology; however, Apel rushes to associate, even though this might seem natural, what Kant calls commerce with contemporary capitalism, and if thought in this way, Kant's framework could hardly be ethically sustainable.[60]

One might be tempted to claim that Kant didn't know about capitalism; more specifically, that he didn't know that the commerce he had in mind would turn out to be the precursor of modern capitalism, or that, if we are to view it

---

[58] Karl-Otto Apel, 'Kant's 'Toward Perpetual Peace' as Historical Prognosis from the Point of View of Moral Duty', in *Perpetual Peace Essays on Kant's Cosmopolitan Ideal*, ed. James Bohman and Matthias Lutz-Bachmann (Cambridge, MA: MIT Press, 1997), 100.

[59] Apel, 'Kant's 'Toward Perpetual Peace', 100.

[60] Apel, 'Kant's 'Toward Perpetual Peace', 100, 'from an ethical perspective, one may arrive at very ambivalent conclusions regarding these developments'. On the other hand, he also recognizes that the economic organizations such as the EU, NAFTA, Mercosur and ASEAN have the strongest potential to prevent wars. On this point, Habermas shares the same view but with different logics. Habermas claims that Kant's thesis on the role of world trade in creating communal ties is *directly wrong*, but it is *indirectly correct*. It is indirectly wrong, since he didn't anticipate capitalism, but he is indirectly right because such a view is only realized after the Second World War and assured by the OECD (Organisation for Economic Co-operation and Development), see Jürgen Habermas, 'Kant's Idea of Perpetual Peace, with the Benefit of Two Hundred Years' Hindsight', in *Perpetual Peace Essays on Kant's Cosmopolitan Ideal*, 122.

historically, Kant therefore contributed to the justification of capitalism. This view on the matter is ahistorical since commerce might well have had another destiny, that is, it may not have developed into the capitalism we know today. Therefore, we have to go back to what Kant understood by trade and commerce. Kant claims that 'it was trade that first brought them into *peaceful relations* with one another and thereby into relationships based on mutual consent, community, and peaceful interactions even with remote peoples', later adding, 'It is the *spirit of trade* [*Handelsgeist*], which cannot coexist with war, which will, sooner or later, take hold of every people'. Kant continues by mentioning that the power of money is the most reliable, no state is able to resist therefore it is able to 'promote the noble peace and, wherever in the world war threatens to break out, to avert it by means of negotiations, just as if they were members of a permanent league'.[61] There is a 'real politics' at play here, for national wealth is the pursuit of all states; more than a legal framework, the power of money is what makes possible a 'permanent league' of states. We need to examine the concept of trade that Kant made in this statement. First, Kant's concept of the state presupposes trade, as we can read in the section on cosmopolitan right in *The Metaphysics of Morals*:

> since possession of the land, on which an inhabitant of the earth can live, can be thought only as possession of a part of a determinate whole, and so as possession of that to which each of them originally has a right, it follows that all nations stand *originally* in a community of land, though not of *rightful* community of possession (*communio*) and so of use of it, or of property in it; instead they stand in a community of possible physical *interaction (commercium)*, that is, in a thoroughgoing relation of each to all the others of *offering to engage in commerce* with any other.[62]

In other words, Kant doesn't see a state as a monad; instead, it must have windows which allow it to communicate with others through commercial activities. The monads, as Leibniz's *Monadology* (1714) tells us, have no windows, but only mirrors; each monad is self-sufficient; it reflects into its mirror the outside world and reflects each reflection until the whole universe is contained therein. The recursivity of the mirrors follows a distributive principle, according to which

---

[61] Kant, 'Towards Perpetual Peace', in *Toward Perpetual Peace and Other Writings on Politics, Peace, and History*, trans. David L. Colclasure, ed. Pauline Kleingeld (New Haven, CT: Yale University Press, 2006), 92; Ak 8:368, italics are original. Kleingeld in her book *Kant and Cosmopolitanism: The Philosophical Ideal of World Citizenship* (Cambridge: Cambridge University 2011), 135, suggests that the term 'spirit of trade' is translated from Montesquieu's 'esprit du commerce' and Kant was inspired by the former's claim that 'Peace is the natural effect of trade'.
[62] Kant, 'The Metaphysics of Morals', 172, Ak. 6:352.

the parts contribute to the whole without losing their individuality – this is the constraint intrinsic to the concept of the individual substance. Leibniz's distributive principle has to be distinguished from Kant's regulative principle,[63] though one has to recognize that both aim at a philosophical organism and that the concept of recursivity is central to both.[64] In other words, we can say that these are similar algorithms with different parameters and functions. Trading as an algorithm is not consistent with the distributive principle, but only with the regulative principle. It presupposes two concepts: reciprocity and community. Reciprocity and community belong to 'Relation' in the table of categories of the *Critique of Pure Reason*.[65] Kant says in the first critique that 'the word community [*Gemeinschaft*] is ambiguous in our language; it can mean the same as *communio* or as *commercium*. We here employ it in the latter sense, as meaning a dynamic community, without which even locational community [*communio spatii*] could never be cognized empirically'.[66] *Commercium* means here sharing, commerce, communication. Reciprocity presupposes the interdependence between agents; community, namely an organic unity, is constituted by reciprocal relations while regulating them simultaneously. In other words, international trade is the concrete form of the reflective judgement contextualized in international relations. This right to trade also falls under what Kant calls cosmopolitan right. It underlines the possibility that 'all nations may unite for the purpose of *creating certain universal laws to regulate the intercourse* they may have with one another'.[67]

We encounter here the problem of self-interest, which could be found in each individual and each institution. Since when we talk about interest, we are more or less talking about empirical inclinations, for example, to earn more profits,

---

[63] Howard Caygill sees the double reflection of the mirror as a form of dynamic principle which Leibniz intended to supplement with the logical and geometrical axioms (*New Physical Hypothesis* (1670)), and that it anticipated Kant's distinction between analytic and synthetic judgments, see Howard Caygill, *Art of Judgment* (Oxford: Blackwell, 1989), 120. Henry Allison suggests that, notwithstanding Kant's claim that the *Critique of Pure Reason* is the 'true apology for Leibniz', the difference between Leibniz and Kant lies more in the third *Critique*. For Leibniz, what is central is 'the doctrine of the pre-established harmony, metaphysically construed as holding between the sensible and intelligible worlds', while for Kant, 'the grounding of the principle of purposiveness is purely immanent, as is befitting its subjective status and connection with reflective judgment'. One cannot ignore the centrality of reflection in Leibniz's *Monadology*, but the individual substance and pre-established harmony limit the way reflection is carried out. See Henry Allison, 'The Critique of Judgment as a 'True Apology for Leibniz'', in *Essays on Kant* (Oxford: Oxford University Press, 2012), 199–200.

[64] Historically, we might also want to trace the influence of the Cambridge Platonist School on Leibniz's organicism, see Hui, *Recursivity and Contingency*, Chapter 1.

[65] In edition A of the *Critique of Pure Reason*, the concept of community is central; in edition B, community comes together with reciprocity, see A215, B260-B261.

[66] Kant, *Critique of Pure Reason*, B260.

[67] Kant, 'The Metaphysics of Morals', 172, Ak. 6:352.

to impose higher tarrifs, to buy cheaper resources, to become more efficient or to have a larger budget. These cannot be the interests of pure reason, because it should be directed towards an interest devoid of any empirical interests, that is, pleasure without interest. How could international trade, one of the greediest businesses, be driven by disinterested interest? Here we encounter again the complex relation between the transcendental and the empirical, because without the empirical, the transcendental is empty, and without the transcendental, the empirical is blind. In other words, even though international trade may be self-interest driven, the transcendental principles could still function behind it. And concerning the progress made by international trade, even though it is not yet a moral step, it is a 'great step toward morality'.[68] In other words, the international trade that Kant has in mind is a speculative heuristic. It is speculative since Kant cannot make a claim that it is for sure realizable, but one could only know by trying out. Again, we are not talking in the discursive mode of truth; we can only speak of morality and perpetual peace in the mode of 'as if'. Any attempt to replace one with the other will lead to a transcendental illusion, and therefore would be bound to fail.[69] Kant's algorithm of peace could be analysed according to the following two premises:

1) In a system of exchange, *reciprocity* regulates the behaviour of individuals; that is, if you want to receive hospitality, then please offer hospitality in return. If you want to behave badly towards others, then you should expect reciprocal treatment.
2) In a system of exchange, the *community* governs the behaviour of each individual. When an individual violates the norm, it will not only damage their reputation but will also be condemned.

How about those who deliberate to break such premises? And how could injustice be avoided? Kant gave the example of East India (Hindustan), where foreign troops were brought to the land under the pretext of establishing trade, but were, in fact, used to introduce oppression to the inhabitants. Kant also gave us the counterexample of how the Chinese and Japanese refused the European aggressors by limiting their *interaction*; for example, China didn't allow any entrance to the country, while Japan only limited its trading with the Dutch. Kant called them wise to shield themselves from the colonizers; indeed, by doing

---

[68] Kant, 'Toward Perpetual Peace', 99, *Ak.* 8:375.
[69] Saner, *Kant's Political Thought*, 56.

so, the European lands were left without winning anything, if not completely failing:

> The worst part of this (or, from the standpoint of a moral judge, the best part) is that they do not even profit from this violence, that all of these trading companies stand near the point of collapse.... The growing prevalence of a (narrower or wider) community among the peoples of the earth has now reached a point at which the violation of right at any *one* place on the earth is felt in *all* places.[70]

The above quote conceals what Kant calls sociability, which assumes at the same time an equilibrium of forces and a vigorous rivalry. The dispersed places become one 'all places', which we could call a cosmopolitan community. Reciprocity and community are inseparable; reciprocity (war is also a form of reciprocity) facilitates the development of community; community regulates the form of reciprocity (from war to peace). We can see that in the above algorithm, there are no predefined rules regulating each individual; one can only find transcendental categories such as reciprocity and community at work.[71] Here lies the *interest* of pure reason. In this vision, international trade, the formal exchange between the states, is the realization of the organic principle driven by moral duty. In this sense, we can understand that Kant's perpetual peace is guaranteed by nature, the great artist [*natura daedala rerum*].[72] Why nature? Kant affirms to us that '[t]he mechanical course of nature visibly reveals a purposive plan to create harmony through discord among people, even against their own will'.[73] We remember that already in his 1784 'Idea for a Universal History with a Cosmopolitan Aim', Kant considers the history of the human species (as the perfect civil union of the human species) as the realization of the hidden plan of nature [*Vollziehung eines verborgenen Plans der Natur*].[74] Kant saw the problem of founding *ius civile* and *ius gentium* on *ius naturale* such as Grotius and Hobbes did; their justification of wars with a fictive anthropological account didn't distinguish the inclination

---

[70] Kant, 'Toward Perpetual Peace', 84; Ak. 8:359–60, italics original.
[71] Therefore, we can see that Kant is not promoting a blind 'free trade', however he is not rejecting free trade or the free market either. His position, thus framed as an organicism, might remind us of the theory of Friedrich Hayek, see Hui, *Machine and Sovereignty*, 103–5.
[72] Kant, 'Toward Perpetual Peace', 85, Ak. 8:360, also quoted by Hannah Arendt, *Lectures on Kant's Political Philosophy* (Chicago, IL: The University of Chicago Press, 1992), 16, 'Thus we find the curious Article in *Perpetual Peace* that establishes a *Besuchsrecht*, the right to visit foreign lands, the right to hospitality, and 'the right of temporary sojourn'. And, in the same treatise, we again find nature, that great artist, as the eventual 'guarantee of perpetual peace''.
[73] Kant, 'Toward Perpetual Peace', 85, Ak. 8:360.
[74] Kant, 'Idea for a Universal History with a Cosmopolitan Aim', in *Political Writings*, 50, Ak. 8:27, 'One can regard the history of the human species in the large as the completion of a hidden plan of nature to bring about an inwardly and, to this end, also an externally perfect state constitution, as the only condition in which it can fully develop all its predispositions in humanity'.

in nature and the reason in nature. With this in mind, we can understand that Kant's vision of perpetual peace is a very logical extension of his concept of organicity which we find from his critical philosophy to political philosophy; it is the realization of the 'technics of nature' in the human community. Perpetual peace and the highest Good are the *telos* of the two different aspects: the *System* reposing on the organic structure and the recursive operation.

Peace is not only presented as a mathematical problem but also as a teleological one. Conflicts are not only overcome through law, but also through one's moral consciousness and will. Kant's algorithm is therefore neither reducible to a mathematical model nor a biological one; it is an autopoietic system which strives for an equilibrium while at the same time anticipating new conflicts. In other words, this equilibrium is always transitional and is never fully realized. We cannot say when perpetual peace will be achievable. This is not to say that Kant's idea remains only theoretical and therefore not practical, which Kant's enemies reproached him for, and which he rephrased in the following manner:

> an enduring universal peace by means of the so-called *balance of power in Europe* is a mere fantasy, like Swift's house that the builder had constructed in such perfect accord with all the laws of equilibrium that it collapsed as soon as a sparrow alighted upon it. But, it will be said, states will never submit to coercive laws of this kind; and a proposal for a universal state of nations to whose power all individual states should voluntarily accommodate themselves so as to obey its laws – however good it may sound in the theory of an Abbe St. Pierre or of a Rousseau still does not hold in practice; and so it has always been ridiculed by great statesmen, and still more by heads of state, as an academic and childish idea emerging from the schools.[75]

As we have already discussed, theory and practice cannot be separated in the manner that occurs with political philosophy and real politics, because without theory, practice alone cannot make any progress (or more precisely, moral progress). Perpetual peace presupposes both the rights and duties of individual humans and individual states; therefore, reciprocity and community of individuals and states are essential. One can imagine that given this dynamic, the system will move towards an equilibrium, though when it will happen exactly remains unknown, or more precisely, unknowable. Retrospectively, one may criticize that such an equilibrium is neither possible nor desirable, because it could simply

---

[75] Kant, 'On the Common Saying: That May Be True in Theory, but It is of No Use in Practice', in Immanuel Kant, *Practical Philosophy*, trans. Mary J. Gregor (Cambridge: Cambridge University Press, 1999), 309; *Ak.* 8:312–3.

mean 'death'. When a system enters a state of equilibrium, it means that there is no more possibility for individuation, and therefore one cannot attribute life to it. In other words, from a thermodynamic point of view, perpetual peace does not mean a happy ending, since it means that there is no more progress, that is, the end of history where the highest Good is achieved. Without having knowledge of thermodynamics, Kant nevertheless understands the necessity of conflicts, for without conflicts, reason will be stagnant. Therefore, perpetual peace as an end might be considered as harmony (i.e. 'the end to all hostilities'[76]), but it is not a pre-established harmony, because such a harmony is not assumed at the beginning; instead, Kant considers conflict central to the possibility of peace and the possibility of morality.

§9. Islands, shores and ships

We attempted to show that the Kantian perpetual peace consists of an algorithm which assumes differences and conflicts, and it attempts to resolve them through reciprocal operation and communal structure. In each new iteration, new conflicts are produced and then resolved. This might sound paradoxical, but it is also rather straightforward. Kant's peace treatise presupposes conflicts in order to avoid wars.[77] In other words, the Kantian algorithm wants to avoid war by generating conflicts in order not to move into an impasse of total destruction while still making moral progress. Three hundred years after Kant's birth, we will have to ask how effective international trade is for achieving perpetual peace, and whether it is still an answer to our global problem. Perhaps the current geopolitical transformation could serve as another key touchstone for evaluating the Kantian peace machine.

Retrospectively, we know that this organic and recursive algorithm was not strong enough to prevent war, and there is a particular bug in it that David Hume calls the 'jealousy of trade'. Hume was addressing two kinds of fear: first, that the money of a nation would be depleted by trade, and second, that trading is harmful

---

[76] Kant, 'Toward Perpetual Peace', 68, Ak. 8:343.
[77] One should be careful reading Kant's comments on wars in the *Critique of Judgment*, where Kant associated war with the sublime and the progress of civilization; it is necessary to contrast it with what he said between 1795 and 1798; see also Arendt, *Kant's Political Philosophy*, 53–4. After quoting Kant's comments on war in the *Critique of Judgment*, Arendt immediately stated, 'These insights of aesthetic and reflective judgment have no practical consequences for action'. If Arendt can say so, it is because she doesn't see the analogical relation between aesthetic judgment and Kant's model of international relations, which is based on the organic structure and reflective operation.

to the nation if it contributes to the improvement and prosperity of neighbours.[78] Hume wanted to show that this kind of jealousy of trade is groundless and that, in fact, trading brought about mutual benefit. Hume's 1758 writing 'Of the Jealousy of Trade' in fact anticipated Adam Smith's 'invisible hand' in *The Theory of Moral Sentiments*, which was published a year later (1759), and Kant's global community in 'Toward Perpetual Peace'. Fichte, in his *The Closed Commercial States*, questioned the effectiveness of trading in relation to peace and immediately spotted the jealousy of trade as a fundamental defect; very much like Hume, Fichte singled out the Dutch, who serve as brokers and manipulate the market, as an example to demonstrate this defect.[79] In the same book, Fichte put forward a nineteenth-century version of 'decoupling', namely, each state must isolate their economic and trade systems from each other. Fichte's treatise was published in 1800, a year after Kant's open criticism against him in his last publication before his death in 1804, the 'Declaration Regarding Fichte's *Wissenschaftslehre* (1799)'. Fichte saw trading as a defect; in fact, for him, Europe would not be able to form a peaceful federation of constitutional republics if economic rivalry continued. Kant didn't agree with this since conflicts and competitions are inevitable,[80] it depends on which algorithm (including the protocols/parameters specified) is effective to prevent wars. For Fichte, international trade shouldn't have been such an important parameter in the algorithm of perpetual peace because it is a fatal bug; instead, Fichte proposes another parameter to replace trade, namely *Wissenschaft*. That is to say, while all states remain commercially closed, they allow the exchange of science and literature between each other. Were Fichte's proposal implemented, would we have had less colonial violence? Fichte was probably right to point out that the 'spirit of trade' is not incompatible with wars, as Kant believes; and indeed, today, we read in the newspapers almost on a daily basis about 'trade wars' and their shocks, which dramatically reversed

---

[78] David Hume, 'Of the Jealousy of Trade', in *Essays, Moral, Political, and Literary* (Indianapolis, IN: Liberty Fund, 1987), 328, 'In opposition to this narrow and malignant opinion, I will venture to assert, that the encrease of riches and commerce in any one nation, instead of hurting, commonly promotes the riches and commerce of all its neighbours; and that a state can scarcely carry its trade and industry very far, where all the surrounding states are buried in ignorance, sloth, and barbarism'.

[79] See Hume, 'Of the Jealousy of Trade', 330, 'The only commercial state, that ought to dread the improvements and industry of their neighbours, is such a one as the DUTCH, who enjoying no extent of land, nor possessing any number of native commodities, flourish only by their being the brokers, and factors, and carriers of others;' also see J. G. Fichte, *The Closed Commercial State*, trans. Anthony Curtis Adler (Albany, NY: State University of New York, 2012), 156, 'The interest in one's own advantage will be joined by an interest in the other's loss. Sometimes a nation will be happy to satisfy the latter without the former, causing pure damages. So it was when the Dutch extirpated all the spice plants that they found beyond the islands set aside for their cultivation, burning part of the harvested spices, just as in war one burns the supplies that cannot be brought along for one's own use'.

[80] Kleingeld, *Kant and Cosmopolitanism*, 144.

the post-Cold War ideology of globalization (i.e. oneness). However, Fichte was truly an 'idealist' in comparison to Kant. Just a half-century after Fichte wrote his own treatise on perpetual peace, the American Black Ships [*kurofune*] knocked on the doors of Japan – the veritable closed commercial state of the late eighteenth century – under the lead of Commodore Matthew Perry in 1853. Japan was threatened to either open the country for trade or enter war. China couldn't escape a similar destiny after the defeat of the two Opium Wars (1839–42, 1856–60). East Asia had to undergo more than a century of modernization in order to catch up with military and technological advancement. They are now participating in the spreading of European modernity throughout the globe. With this history in mind, could we refuse Kant's perpetual peace according to our tragic experience from the nineteenth century up to now?

A true Kantian wouldn't subscribe to the defeat of Kant's perpetual peace. He or she might argue that algorithms depend on their supporting technical apparatus; therefore, the fact that the machines associated with the algorithm went wrong doesn't mean that the algorithm itself went astray. We know well that many technical apparatuses go awry not because the theory underlying them doesn't work but rather because certain technical elements (trade, in this case) did not fully function as expected. The universal still lies ahead of us, and the search for it is guided by the regulative principle. Should this be the case, it will demand our examination of the technical parts of the proposed solution. If we return to our previous discussion on the 'planetary governance' of a superintelligence, we might want to ask if contemporary technology could replace trade in our time, for like trading in the time of Kant, technology today implies automatized communication and community. More than the peace algorithm based on international trading, the algorithms and communication protocols (from centralized to decentralized and distributed) today could be finely calibrated and greatly improved. How could they provide us with a new strategy towards perpetual peace beyond their use as mere communication tools?[81] The Kantian legacy offers both inspiration and insight into the limitations

---

[81] The Japanese philosopher and critic Hiroki Azuma, in his book *Philosophy of the Tourist*, trans. John D. Person (Falmouth: Urbanomic, 2023) took up Kant's task and suggests that tourism might be a way to conceive of peace. Azuma's argument, on the one hand, inherits Kant's assumptions; for example, the recognition of the individual and the organic structure of organization, borrowing from network theory, he perceives a tourist as a packet routing in the information network. On the other hand, Azuma doesn't prioritize a network of balanced power or perfect delivery, but rather what he calls misdelivery, namely contingent encounters. Another Japanese philosopher and critic, Kojin Karatani takes up the concept of the world republic and suggests extending the concept of exchange from commercial goods to the exchange of sovereignty, see Kojin Karatani, *The Structure of World History: From Modes of Production to Modes of Exchange*, trans. Michael K. Bourdaghs (Durham, NC: Duke University Press, 2014).

of contemporary machines. Even though we have refused the possibility that a superintelligence can take us to perpetual peace, and we must set limits for machines, they continue to occupy a central role for the future of peace, such as it was the case with the trading ships of the Hanseatic League, of the Baltic traders or the Dutch and British traders, which Kant saw at the harbour of Königsberg. Today, we are in a different kind of competition and with different institutions, no longer only marine forces and ships, but also air forces, space technologies, data centers, cloud servers and AI. Humanity is struggling to go beyond its terrestrial confines and is turning the earth into a spacecraft among many others. Technological acceleration speeds up the obsolescence of the human and its relation to the earth, consequently throwing a philosophy concerning human and nature into melancholia. With artificial intelligence, warfare is going to take a different form: AI weapons, robots capable of armed action, and precise missile attacks launched from outer space. At the beginning of this chapter, we examined the effort to use AI to predict and mediate conflicts, but we also know that it doesn't lead to peace but more warfare. Indeed, prediction has become the source of war, either predicting potential terrorists or predicting future conflicts; we can imagine that in the future, not only international politics could be subsumed to prediction, but all socio-political problems will also be associated with predictions of different kinds. The future warfare could happen between drones, military robots and automatic offence/defence systems, but for sure, they will all lead to the massive destruction of human and non-human living beings. Where, then, can we locate machines of peace even if we only see machines of war?

As Kant has shown, conflicts are inevitable; the new machines of war will continue postponing perpetual peace by bringing in new conflicts – just as after the atomic bomb, we also now have AI warfare competition. At the moment of this writing, China just launched DeepSeek as a competitor to ChatGPT and similar products, to signal that China is capable of participating in the AI competition even under the sanctions against importing advanced microchips; it is not only a competition between two companies but also a competition between the so-called 'sovereign AI'. DeepSeek will only serve as the beginning of this AI competition and conflict. An even more explicit example is that in November 2024, the Russian army launched their hypersonic missile Oreshnik, which boasted a strong manoeuvrability and a navigation system, and with which the Russian president Vladimir Putin could claim that it could rival the destructive power of nuclear weapons; and one shouldn't also forget what Putin had already said on 1 September 2017 to the schoolchildren: 'whoever leads in AI will dominate the world'.[82] It doesn't mean that nuclear bombs become obsolete, but rather that certain kinds of destruction are more favourable than others since, in comparison, they might bring more benefits than harms to the party that uses them. It is doubtful whether such homogeneous and vertical competition alone can bring about peace. Yet we must remember that conflict is not necessarily detrimental – there may exist an algorithm capable of regulating conflicts, one that avoids war by seeking the universal while preserving and cultivating plurality; now, not only philosophers but also engineers and artists can join forces to look for such an algorithm. If the algorithm of international trading didn't work out, the regulative principle concerning the whole and parts might still hold. However, we have to bear in mind that its application and theorization are perhaps beyond Kant's own expectations. Reflective judgement as a heuristic searching for a *telos* beyond the linear relation between means and ends has been widely adopted after Kant, not only for peace but also for war. This may sound perplexing if not ironic, but it is nonetheless a demonstration of how philosophy is continually challenged and renewed in order to remain adequate to its time. For example, the regulative principle finds its place in the work of Carl von Clausewitz, the Prussian military theorist. Clausewitz was two generations after Kant and a reader of Kant, Fichte, Hegel and Schelling. Ironically, the title of Clausewitz's *opus magnum*, *On War*, might appear to be on the opposite side of Kant, who quests for *No War*. Howard Caygill convincingly shows that Clausewitz's *On War* should be read as a book on the resistance against applying pregiven rules in wars (i.e. determinative judgement), but rather it is an 'intensification of Kant's reflective judgement',[83] where the 'purposiveness without purpose' finds its application beyond aesthetics in the strategy of attack. For this reason, Caygill suggests that *On War* should have been named *Critique of Military Reason*.[84] Retrospectively, Kant's reflective judgement becomes the essential part of the organismic paradigm, which not only has its expression and value in natural sciences and technologies, but also in warfare and capital accumulation (e.g. the intimacy between organicism/cybernetics and Friedrich

---

[82] AP, 'Putin: Leader in Artificial Intelligence Will Rule World', https://apnews.com/article/bb5628f2a7424a10b3e38b07f4eb90d4.

[83] See Howard Caygill, *On Resistance: A Philosophy of Defiance* (London: Bloomsbury, 2013), 18, '*On War* is in no respect an apology for the workings of reason in history, but is rather an intensification of Kant's reflective judgment in which the case *resists* the application of a rule, puncturing its legitimacy and providing an occasion for a meditation on the impact of chance and enmity on reason'.

[84] Caygill, *On Resistance*, 16.

Hayek's theory of the market[85]). The development and application of cybernetics since the second half of the twentieth century call for the end of this paradigm of thinking (end also in the sense of realization and completion) as well as a new condition of philosophizing after the organic. Where and how could the Kantian idea still find its place in our contemporary situation is a task that we have to examine, to elaborate on the condition of philosophizing of our time, which certainly will have to take a different form from what Kant analysed for his time.[86] Kant left us different threads to think about machines today as we have outlined in this work: intelligence, morality and peace. All these machines are grounded in an epistemological shift from machine to organism, which is biologically and philosophically expressed as an 'epigenesis of reason'. Whether Kant's algorithm still works and how could it be modified will demand a thorough critique of the epistemological foundations of his critical philosophy.

The Kantian peace machine contains such an imperative: 'There should be no war [*Es soll kein Krieg sein*]'. This remains an essential task for machines of the twenty-first century. For sure, we saw wars after Kant, wars among religions, wars among philosophical schools, wars among the bellicose heads, and we now are witnessing wars and we will continue witnessing probably even more wars because the song of *belligerati* is echoing throughout the planet. The recurrence of war doesn't mean that a perpetual peace is not desirable; on the contrary, like all utopians, its not-yet-coming-into-being is the condition of this desire. Because once an object of desire is attained, the faculty of desire would collapse since the object of desire no longer exists; namely, its unattainability is the condition of the will, for one only wills what one lacks. We have to reaffirm with Kant: conflicts are necessary, but wars are not unavoidable. Reason marches towards its maturity with a problematic mode of existence. Perpetual peace in politics is equivalent to the highest Good in morality, for one cannot show what exactly it looks like, and one cannot demonstrate that it is impossible, but without it, the preservation of reason through the human wouldn't be possible. Thus, Kant concludes the 'Doctrine of Right' of *The Metaphysics of Morals* with the following sentence:

---

[85] Friedrich Hayek, *Law, Legislation and Liberty. A New Statement of the Liberal Principles of Justice and Political Economy* (London: Routledge, 1982), xviii. "It was largely the growth of cybernetics and the related subjects of information and system theory which persuaded me that expression other than those which I habitually used may be more read- ily comprehensible to the contemporary reader."

[86] This is the task that *Recursivity and Contingency* (2019), *Art and Cosmotechnics* (2021) and *Machine and Sovereignty* (2024) endeavor to clarify.

> it is no longer a question of whether perpetual peace is really possible or not, or whether we are not perhaps mistaken in our theoretical judgement if we assume that it is. On the contrary, we must simply act as if it could really come about (which is perhaps impossible) and turn our efforts towards realising it and towards establishing that constitution which seems most suitable for this purpose (perhaps that of republicanism in all states, individually and collectively).[87]

The search for perpetual peace is another synonym of the *epigenesis* of reason, for reason will have to expand towards the universal unveiled through its self-awakening; this expansion transgresses the limit of theoretical reason, defines the new territory of practical reason, and stretches into the aesthetic and political realms. The search for perpetual peace is analogous to inquiring into the teleology of humanity, for the cosmopolitan end of the human being implies a heuristic which is not given as such but possible within the boundary of mere reason. The Kant machine is a machine of reason which sets boundaries for itself in order to expand with prudence; it orients through subjective means by the 'feeling of a need which is inherent in reason itself [*Gefühl des der Vernunft eigenen Bedürfnisses*]', even though one might not have enough theoretical knowledge to make the judgement;[88] it proceeds by actively negating the empirical inclinations and self-interests in order to see through the marine fogs over the ocean, the danger and hope beyond the island of pure reason. The machine overcomes its own limit through the mediation of human *intelligentia*, physical labours, and now all kinds of data (including those of humans and non-humans, terrestrial and extra-terrestrial), with which today's autonomous vessels are able to sail in the ocean and outer space without the intervention of humans. Kant, however, didn't consider it his task to analyse further the identity and dialectics between the progress of machines and the progress of reason, since his understanding of the machine was still limited to those automata of Jacques de Vaucanson and alike, which are not at all comparable to contemporary machinery. Moreover, an organology remained implicit in his thought and was largely subordinated to the concept of the organism. Contemporary cybernetic machines have already exceeded Kant's imagination, and the overlaps between the working principles of these machines and Kant's philosophy brought us something equally stimulating and disturbing. Given the biological/teleological inspiration of Kant's critical philosophy, one is tempted to ask if machines could also become critical? The question – or more precisely, the invitation posed by contemporary machines

---

[87] Kant, 'The Metaphysics of Morals', 174, *Ak.* 6:354.
[88] Kant, 'What is Orientation in Thinking (1786)', in *Political Writings*, 240; *Ak.* 8:136.

– remains open; yet it demands the intervention of reason, lest we fall into *Schwärmerei*, ironically in the name of humanity. The critical philosophy which identified itself on the island and keeps it away from the terrifying waves will have to set off again into the infinite ocean in order to explore new territories. What is ahead of it is yet to be known, and what Kant might say about it will have to be updated beyond his critical philosophy – a task that is urgently needed; however, it is neither a matter of rejecting Kant nor of affirming him, since the Kant machine is at the same time obsolete and actual. Though its epistemological foundation has to be re-examined in light of the dominance of cybernetic machines, it also anticipated the limits of the cybernetic machines and illusions that they brought about. One thing of which we can be sure is that behind the marine fogs hide the seductions of dogmatists and sceptics, idealists and realists, as well as the attacks from sea rovers and bellicose heads, but there are neither detours of escape, nor is there comfort in running ashore for safety's sake,[89] instead they must be conflicted with reason.

> Forever will war be no more,
> If we heed the words of the wise;
> All men would live at peace,
> All but the philosophers.
> *Auf ewig ist der Krieg vermieden;*
> *Befolgt man, was der Weise spricht,*
> *Dann halten alle Menschen Frieden,*
> *Allein die Philosophen nicht.*[90]

---

[89] As Kant would say about Hume, see Manfred Kuehn, *Kant: A Biography* (Cambridge: Cambridge University Press, 2001), 264.
[90] Abraham Gotthelf Kästner's epigram titled 'Vom ewigen Frieden', cited by Saner, *Kant's Political Philosophy*, 233. Trans. by Yuk Hui.

Bibliography

Ackley, David H., Geoffrey E. Hinton and Terrence J. Sejnowski. 'A Learning Algorithm for Boltzmann Machines'. *Cognitive Science* 9, no. 1 (1985): 147–69.

Agamben, Giorgio. *The Use of Bodies*. Translated by Adam Kotsko. Stanford, CA: Stanford University Press, 2016.

Agre, Philip. *Computation and Human Experience*. Cambridge: Cambridge University Press, 1997.

Aigner, Franziska. *Kant and Technics. From the Critique of Pure Reason to the Opus Postumum*. London: Bloomsbury, 2024.

Allen, Colin Gary Varner and Jason Zinser. 'Prolegomena to any future artificial moral agent'. *Journal of Experimental & Theoretical Artificial Intelligence* 12, no. 3 (2010): 251–61.

Allison, Henry E. *Essays on Kant*. Oxford: Oxford University Press, 2012.

Allison, Henry E. 'Kant and the Two Dogmas of Rationalism'. In *A Companion to Rationalism*, edited by Alan Nelson, 69–88. Oxford: Blackwell, 2005.

Allison, Henry E. 'Kant's Critique of Spinoza'. In *The Philosophy of Baruch Spinoza*, edited by Richard Kennington, 199–277. Washington, DC: Catholic University of America Press, 1980.

Anderson, Chris. 'The End of Theory: The Data Deluge Makes the Scientific Method Obsolete'. *Wired*, 2008. https://www.wired.com/2008/06/pb-theory/.

Angelini, Andrea. 'Comparing Artificial, Animal and Scientific Intelligence: A Dialogue with Giuseppe Longo'. *Theory, Culture & Society* 39, no. 7–8 (2022): 71–97.

AP News. 'Putin: Leader in Artificial Intelligence Will Rule World'. https://apnews.com/article/bb5628f2a7424a10b3e38b07f4eb90d4.

Apel, Karl-Otto. 'Kant's 'Toward Perpetual Peace' as Historical Prognosis from the Point of View of Moral Duty'. In *Perpetual Peace Essays on Kant's Cosmopolitan Ideal*, edited by James Bohman and Matthias Lutz-Bachmann, 79–112. Cambridge, MA: MIT Press, 1997.

Arendt, Hannah. *Lectures on Kant's Political Philosophy*. Chicago, IL: The University of Chicago Press, 1982.

Arendt, Hannah. *The Human Condition*. Chicago, IL: The University of Chicago Press, 1998.

Aristotle, *Magna Moralia*. Translated by W. D. Ross. Oxford: Clarendon Press, 1915.

Asimov, Isaac. 'Run Around'. In *I, Robot*, 20-33. New York: Doubleday, 1950.

Azuma, Hiroki. *Philosophy of the Tourist*. Translated by John D. Person. Falmouth: Urbanomic, 2023.

Baumgarten, Alexander. *Aesthetica* (Latin-German). Hamburg: Felix Meiner, 2007.

Benanti, Paolo. 'Algorethics: The Timeless Values of Religion and Their Irreplaceable Contribution to the Humane and Peaceful Development of Artificial Intelligence (2022)'. https://www.paolobenanti.com/post/algorethics-g20.

Bengio, Yoshua, Yann LeCun and Geoffrey Hinton. 'Deep Learning for AI', Turing Lecture 2021. *Communications of the ACM,* 2021. https://cacm.acm.org/research/deep-learning-for-ai/.

Brandt, Reinhard. 'Der Zirkel im dritten Abschnitt von Kants Grundlegung zur Metaphysik der Sitten'. In *Kant. Analysen - Probleme – Kritik,* edited by H. Oberer and G. Seel, 169–91. Würzburg: Königshausen & Neumann, 1988.

Brooks, Rodney. *Cambrian Intelligence: The Early History of the New AI.* Cambridge, MA: MIT Press, 1999.

Browning, Jacob and Yann LeCun. 'What AI Can Tell Us About Intelligence'. *Noema,* 2022. https://www.noemamag.com/what-ai-can-tell-us-about-intelligence/.

Canguilhem, Georges. *Knowledge of Life.* Translated by Stefanos Geroulanos and Daniela Ginsburg. New York: Fordham, 2008.

Cantwell Smith, Brian. *The Promise of Artificial Intelligence: Reckoning and Judgment.* Cambridge, MA: MIT Press, 2019.

Casetta, Elena. 'Preformation vs. Epigenesis: Inspiration and Haunting Within and Outside Contemporary Philosophy of Biology'. *Journal of Aesthetics* 74 (2020): 119–38.

Cassirer, Ernst. *Kant's Life and Thought.* Translated by James Haden. New Haven, CT: Yale University Press, 1983.

Caygill, Howard. *Art of Judgement.* Oxford: Blackwell, 1989.

Caygill, Howard. *On Resistance. A Philosophy of Defiance.* London: Bloomsbury, 2013.

Chaitin, Gregory. 'Leibniz, Information, Math and Physics', 2005. http://arxiv.org/abs/math/0306303.

Chaitin, Gregory. " An Algorithmic God", Inference: International Review of Science, Vol.1 No.4 (October 2015), https://inference-review.com/article/an-algorithmic-god#

Chiang, Ted. 'Chatgpt is a Blurry Jpeg of the Web'. *New York Times,* 2023. https://www.newyorker.com/tech/annals-of-technology/chatgpt-is-a-blurry-jpeg-of-the-web.

Cohen, Hermann. *Kants Theorie der Erfahrung.* Berlin: Ferd. Dümmlers, 1885.

Covell, Charles. *Kant and the Law of Peace : A Study in the Philosophy of International Law and International Relations.* London: Palgrave Macmillan, 1998.

Darwell, Stephen. *Modern Moral Philosophy: From Grotius to Kant.* Cambridge: Cambridge University Press, 2023.

Dawid, Philip and Donald Gillies. 'A Bayesian Analysis of Hume's Argument Concerning Miracles'. *The Philosophical Quarterly* 39, no. 154 (1989): 57–65.

Deleuze, Gilles. *Kant's Critical Philosophy.* Translated by Hugh Tomlinson and Barbara Habberjam. London: The Athlone Press, 1984.

Descartes, René. *The Philosophical Writings of Descartes,* Vol. 1. Cambridge: Cambridge University Press, 1985.

Dreyfus, Hubert. *Skillful Coping: Essays on the Phenomenology of Everyday Perception and Action*, edited by Mark Wrathall. Oxford: Oxford University Press, 2014.

Dreyfus, Hubert. *What Computers Cannot Do. A Critique of Artificial Reason*. New York: Harper & Row, 1972.

Dreyfus, Hubert. 'Why Heideggerian AI Failed and How Fixing It Would Require Making It More Heideggerian'. *Artificial Intelligence* 171, no. 18 (2007): 1137–60.

Dupuy, Jean-Pierre. *The Mechanization of the Mind: On the Origins of Cognitive Science*. Translated by M. B. DeBevoise. Princeton, NJ: Princeton University Press, 2000.

Evans, Richard. 'The Apperception Engine'. In *Kant and Artificial Intelligence*, edited by Hyeongjoo Kim and Dieter Schönecker, 39–104. Berlin: De Gruyter, 2022.

Fenves, Peter. *Late Kant: Towards Another Law of the Earth*. London: Rouledge, 2003.

Fichte, J. G. *The Closed Commercial State*. Translated by Anthony Curtis Adler. Albany, NY: State University of New York, 2012.

Foucault, Michel. 'What is Enlightenment?' In *The Foucault Reader*, edited by Paul Rabinow, 32–50. New York: Pantheon Books, 1984.

Griffing, Harold. 'J. H. Lambert: A Study in the Development of the Critical Philosophy'. *The Philosophical Review* 2, no. 1 (1893): 54–62. https://doi.org/10.2307/2176069.

Guyer, Paul. *Kant on the Rationality of Morality*. Cambridge: Cambridge University Press, 2019.

Habermas, Jürgen. 'Kant's Idea of Perpetual Peace, with the Benefit of Two Hundred Years' Hindsight'. In *Perpetual Peace Essays on Kant's Cosmopolitan Ideal*, edited by James Bohman and Matthias Lutz-Bachmann, 113–154. Cambridge, MA: MIT Press, 1997

Haugland, John. *Artificial Intelligence: The Very Idea*. Cambridge, MA: MIT Press, 1989.

Hayek, Friedrich, *Law, Legislation and Liberty. A New Statement of the Liberal Principles of Justice and Political Economy*. London: Routledge, 1982.

Hegel, G. W. F. *Outlines of the Philosophy of Right*. Translated by T. M. Knox. Oxford: Oxford University Press, 2008.

Heidegger, Martin. *Being and Time*. Translated by John Macquarrie and Edward Robinson. New York: Harper & Row, 1962.

Heidegger, Martin. *Schelling's Treatise on the Essence of Human Freedom*. Translated by Joan Stambaugh, Athens, OH: Ohio University Press, 1985.

Henrich, Dieter. *The Unity of Reason Essays on Kant's Philosophy*. Cambridge, MA: Harvard University Press, 1994.

Hobbes, Thomas. *Leviathan*. Indianapolis, IN: Hackett, 1994.

Hui, Yuk. *Art and Cosmotechnics*. Minneapolis, MN: University of Minnesota Press/e-flux, 2021.

Hui, Yuk. *Machine and Sovereignty. For a Planetary Thinking*. Minneapolis, MN: University of Minnesota Press, 2024.

Hui, Yuk. *On the Existence of Digital Objects*. Minneapolis, MN: University of Minnesota Press, 2016.

Hui, Yuk. *Recursivity and Contingency*. London: Rowman and Littlefield, 2019.

Hume, David. *A Treatise of Human Nature: Vol. 1: Text*. Oxford: Clarendon Press, 2007.

Hume, David. *Essays, Moral, Political, and Literary*. Indianapolis, IN: Liberty Fund, 1987.

Huneman, Philippe. *Métaphysique et biologie Kant et la constitution du concept d'organisme*. Paris: Kimé, 2008.

Illetterati, Luca. 'Teleological Judgment: Between Technique and Nature'. In *Kant's Theory of Biology*, edited by Ina Goy and Eric Watkins, 81-98. Berlin: De Gruyter, 2014.

James, William. *Pragmatism: A New Name for Some Old Ways of Thinking*. Cambridge, MA: Harvard University Press, 1907.

John. *Revelation*. https://web.mit.edu/jywang/www/cef/Bible/NIV/NIV_Bible/REV+8.html.

Kalimtzis, Kostas. *An Inquiry into the Philosophical Concept of Scholê. Leisure as a Political End*. London: Bloomsbury, 2017.

Kant, Immanuel. *Anthropology from a Pragmatic Point of View*. Translated by Robert B. Louden. Cambridge: Cambridge University Press, 2006.

Kant, Immanuel. *Briefwechsel*. Edted by Otto Schöndörffer. Hamburg: Felix Meiner Verlag, 1972.

Kant, Immanuel. *Conflict of the Faculties*. Translated by Mary J. Gregor. New York: Abaris Books, 1979.

Kant, Immanuel. *Critique of Judgement*. Translated by James Creed Meredith and Nicholas Walker. Oxford: Oxford University Press, 2007.

Kant, Immanuel. *Critique of Practical Reason*. Translated by Werner S. Pluhar. Indianapolis, IN: Hackett, 2002.

Kant, Immanuel. *Critique of Pure Reason*. Translated by Werner S. Pluhar. Indianapolis, IN: Hackett Publishing, 1996.

Kant, Immanuel. *Gesammelte Schriften*. Herausgegeben von der Königlich Preußischen Akademie der Wissenschaften. 29 vols. Berlin: Walter de Gruyter, 1900–.

Kant, Immanuel. *Der alte Kant: Hasse's Schrift – Letzte Äußerungen Kants*. Edited by Artur Buchenau and Gerhard Lehmann. Berlin: Walter de Gruyter, 1925.

Kant, Immanuel. *Groundwork for the Metaphysics of Moral*. Translated by Allen W. Wood. New Haven, CT: Yale University Press, 2002.

Kant, Immanuel. *Kant's Idea for a Universal History with a Cosmopolitan Aim. A Critical Guide*. Edited by Amélie Oksenberg Rorty and James Schmidt. Cambridge: Cambridge University Press, 2009.

Kant, Immanuel. *Lectures on Logic*. Translated by J. Michael Young. Cambridge: Cambridge University Press, 1992.

Kant, Immanuel. *Political Writings*. Translated by H. B. Nisbet, edited by H. S. Reiss. Cambridge: Cambridge University Press, 1991.

Kant, Immanuel. *Practical Philosophy*. Translated by Mary J. Gregor. Cambridge: Cambridge University Press, 1999.

Kant, Immanuel. *Prolegomena to Any Future Metaphysics*. Translated by Gary Hatfield. Cambridge: Cambridge University Press, 2004.

Kant, Immanuel. *Religion within the Boundaries of Mere Reason*. Translated by Allen Wood and Georege di Giovanni. Cambridge: Cambridge University Press, 1998.

Kant, Immanuel. *The Metaphysics of Morals*. Translated by Mary Gregor. Cambridge: Cambridge University Press, 1991.

Kant, Immanuel. *Theoretical philosophy, 1755-1770*. Translated by David Walford and Ralf Meerbote. Cambridge: Cambridge University Press, 1992.

Kant, Immanuel. *Theoretical Philosophy after 1781*. Translated by Hatfield et al., edited by Henry Allison et al. Cambridge: Cambridge University Press, 2009.

Karatani, Kojin. *The Structure of World History: From Modes of Production to Modes of Exchange*. Translated by Michael K. Bourdaghs. Durham, NC: Duke University Press, 2014.

Kelly, Jack. 'Three Key Misconceptions in the Debate about AI and Existential Risk', 2024. https://thebulletin.org/2024/07/three-key-misconceptions-in-the-debate-about-ai-and-existential-risk/.

Kleingeld, Pauline. *Kant and Cosmopolitanism The Philosophical Ideal of World Citizenship*. Cambridge: Cambridge University Press, 2011.

Kojève, Alexandre. *Kant*. Paris: Gallimard, 1973.

Korsgaard, Christine. *The Sources of Normativity*. Cambridge: Cambridge University Press, 2010.

Kuehn, Manfred. *Kant A Biography*. Cambridge: Cambridge University Press, 2001.

Latour, Bruno and G. Teil, 'The Hume Machine. Can Associations Networks Do More than Formal Rules?' *Stanford Humanities Review* 4, no. 2 (1995): 47–66.

LeCun, Yann. "How Could Machines Learn as Efficiently as Animals and Humans?"(2017), https://www.ias.edu/events/lecun-publiclecture

Lehmann, Gerhard. 'Technik der Natur'. In *Beiträge zur Geschichte und Interpretation der Philosophie Kants*, 289–94. Berlin: De Gruyter, 1969.

Leibniz, G. W. *Discourse on Metaphysics and Other Essays*. Translated by Daniel Garber and Roger Ariew. Indianapolis, IN: Hackett, 1989.

Leibniz, G. W. *Philosophical Papers and Letters*, edited by Leroy E. Loemker. Dordrecht: D. Reidel, 1969.

Lenoir, Timothy. *The Strategy of Life*. Dordrecht: D. Reidel, 1982.

Longuenesse, Béatrice. *Kant on Human Standpoint*. Cambridge: Cambridge University Press, 2009.

Lyotard, Jean-François. *Leçons sur l'Analytique du sublime. Kant, Critique de la faculté de jugerm §23–29*. Paris: Klincksieck, 2015.

Manchester, Paula. 'Kant's Conception of Architectonic in its Historical Context'. *Journal of the History of Philosophy* 41, no. 2 (2003): 187–207.

Marx, Karl. *Capital Vol. 1*. Translated by Ben Fowkes. London: Penguin Books, 1990.

McCarthy, John, Marvin Minsky, Nathaniel L. Rochester and Claude E. Shannon, 'A Proposal for the Dartmouth Summer Research Project on Artificial Intelligence'. *AI Magazine* 27, no. 4 (1955): 12–14.

McDowell, John. *World and Mind*. Cambridge, MA: Harvard University Press, 1996.

Meillassoux, Quentin. *After Finitude: An Essay on the Necessity of Contingency.* Translated by Ray Brassier. London: Continuum, 2008.

Mensch, Jennifer. *Kant's Organicism.* Chicago, IL: The University of Chicago Press, 2013.

Minsky, Marvin. 'Steps toward Artificial Intelligence'. *Proceedings of the IRE* 49, no. 1 (1961): 8–30.

Morris, William. *The Collected Works of William Morris.* Cambridge: Cambridge University Press, 2012.

Neiman, Susan. *The Unity of Reason. Reading Kant.* Oxford: Oxford University Press, 1994.

Newell, Allen. 'Intellectual Issues in the History of Artificial Intelligence' DTIC ADA125318. Fort Belvoir, VA: Defense Technical Information Center, 1982; published in *The Study of Information : Interdisciplinary Messages*, edited by Fritz Machlup and Una Mansfield, 187-227. New York: John Wiley&Son, 1983.

Nietzsche, Friedrich. *Beyond Good and Evil Prelude to a Philosophy of the Future.* Translated by Judith Norman. Cambridge: Cambridge University Press, 2002.

Nietzsche, Friedrich. *On the Genealogy of Morality.* Translated by Carol Diethe. Cambridge: Cambridge University Press, 2006.

Ostaric, Lara. *The Critique of Judgment and the Unity of Kant's Critical System.* Cambridge: Cambridge University Press, 2023.

Palmquist, Stephen R., *Kant and Mysticism. Critique as the Experience of Baring All in Reason's Light.* Lanham MD: Lexington, 2019.

Pearl, Judea and Dana McKenzie. *The Book of Why: The New Science of Cause and Effect.* New York: Basic Books, 2018.

Plato. *Parmenides.* In *Complete Works of Plato*, 359-397

Plato. *Phaedrus.* In *Complete Works of Plato*, edited by John M. Cooper and D. S. Hutchinson, 506-556. Indianapolis, IN: Hackett, 1997.

Powers, Thomas M. 'Machines and Moral Reasoning'. *Philosophy Now,* 2009. https://philosophynow.org/issues/72/Machines_and_Moral_Reasoning.

Quarfood, Marcel. *Transcendental Idealism and the Organism: Essays on Kant.* Stockholm: Almqvist & Wiksell International, 2004.

Reichl, Pavel. 'Kant's Herder Review: Analogical Inference, Indirect Cognition, and Philosophical Style'. In *The Court of Reason. Proceedings of the 13th International Kant Congress*, edited by Beatrix Himmelmann and Camilla Serck-Hanssen, 2015-2022. Berlin: De Gruyter, 2021.

Richards, Robert J. 'Kant and Blumenbach on the *Bildungstrieb*: A Historical Misunderstanding'. *Studies in History and Philosophy of Biological and Biomedical Sciences* 31, no. 1 (2000): 11–32.

Riskin, Jessica. *The Restless Clock.* Chicago, IL: The University of Chicago Press, 2016.

Rousseau, Jean-Jacques. 'Abstract and Judgement of Saint-Pierre's Project for Perpetual Peace'. Translated by C. E. Vaughan. In *Rousseau on International Relations*, edited by Stanley Hoffmann and David P. Fidler, 53-100. Oxford: Oxford University Press, 1991.

Rousseau, Jean-Jacques. *The Social Contract and the First and Second Discourses*. New Haven, CT and London: Yale University Press, 2002.

Saner, Hans. *Kant's Political Thought: Its Origin and Development*. Chicago, IL: The University of Chicago Press, 1973.

Santozki, Ulrike. *Die Bedeutung antiker Theorien für die Genese und Systematik von Kants Philosophie*. Berlin: De Gruyter, 2006.

Schelling, F. W. J. *Philosophical Investigations into the Essence of Human Freedom*. Translated by Jeff Love and Johannes Schmidt. Albany, NY: State University of New York, 2006.

Schmidhuber, Juergen. 'Gödel Machines: Self-Referential Universal Problem Solvers Making Provably Optimal Self-Improvements', 2003. https://arxiv.org/abs/cs/0309048.

Schmidhuber, Jürgen. 'Deep Learning in Neural Networks: An Overview'. *Neural Networks* 61 (2015): 85–117.

Schmitt, Carl. *The Concept of the Political*. Translated by George Schwab. Chicago, IL: The University of Chicago Press, 1996.

Searle, John R. 'Minds, Brains, and Programs'. *Behavioral and Brain Sciences* 3, no. 3 (1980): 417–57.

Sejnowski, Terrence J. *The Deep Learning Revolution*. Cambridge, MA: MIT Press, 2018.

Simondon, Gilbert. *On the Mode of Existence of Technical Objects*. Translated by Cecile Malaspina and John Rogove. Minneapolis, MN: Univocal, 2017.

Simondon, Gilbert. *Sur la Philosophie*. Paris: PUF, 2016.

Sloan, Phillip R. 'Performing the Categories: Eighteenth-Century Generation Theory and the Biological Roots of Kant's A Priori'. *Journal of the History of Philosophy* 40, no. 2 (2002): 229–53.

Solomonoff, Ray. 'A Formal Theory of Inductive Inference, Part I'. *Information and Control* 7, no.1(March 1964): 1–22.

Solomonoff, Ray. 'A Formal Theory of Inductive Inference, Part II'. *Information and Control* 7, no.2 (March 1964): 224–54.

Solomonoff, Ray. *A Preliminary Report on a General Theory of Inductive Inference'*. Cambridge, MA: Zator Company, 1960.

Solomonoff, Ray. 'The Discovery of Algorithmic Probability'. *Journal of Computer and System Sciences* 55, no. 1 (1997): 73–88.

Stiegler, Bernard. *Technics and Time, 3 Cinematic Time and the Question of Malaise*. Translated by Stephen Barker. Stanford, CA: Stanford University Press, 2010.

Strickland, Eliza. 'OpenAI's Moonshot: Solving the AI Alignment Problem'. *IEEE Spectrum*, August 2023. https://spectrum.ieee.org/the-alignment-problem-openai.

Strauss, Leo. *The City and Man*. Chicago, IL: Chicago University Press, 1964.

The Guardian. "The Machine Did It Coldly': Israel Used AI to Identify 37,000 Hamas Targets', 3 April 2024. https://www.theguardian.com/world/2024/apr/03/israel-gaza-ai-database-hamas-airstrikes.

Turing, Alan. *The Essential Turing: Seminal Writings in Computing, Logic, Philosophy, Artificial Intelligence, and Artificial Life: Plus The Secrets of Enigma*. Edited by B. Jack Copeland. Oxford: Clarendon Press, 2004.

Van Dyck, Karen and Souleymane Bachir Diagne. 'In Conversation. Karen Van Dyck speaks with Souleymane Bachir Diagne: Mutuality and Unexpected Collaboration in Translation'. *The Translator* 29, no. 4 (2023): 408–20.

Vuillemin, Jules. *Physique et métaphysique kantiennes*. Paris: PUF, 1987.

Weatherby, Leif. *Transplanting the Metaphysical Organ: German Romanticism between Leibniz and Marx*. New York: Fordham University Press, 2016.

Weber, Andreas and Francisco J. Varela, 'Life after Kant: Natural Purposes and the Autopoietic Foundations of Biological Individuality'. *Phenomenology and the Cognitive Sciences* 1 (2002): 97–125.

Weizenbaum, Joseph. *Computer Power and Human Reason: From Judgement to Calculation*. New York: Freeman, 1976.

White, Joel. 'How Does One Cosmotheoretically Respond to the Heat Death of the Universe?' *Open Philosophy* 6, no. 1 (2023): 2022–33.

Whitehead, Alfred North. *Process and Reality*. Edited by D. R. Griffin and D. W. Sherburne. New York: Free Press, 1978.

Wiener, Norbert. *Cybernetics or Control and Communication in the Animal and the Machine*. Cambridge, MA: MIT Press, 1961.

Wilczek, Frank. 'The Unity of Intelligence'. In *Possible Minds. Twenty-Five Ways of Looking at AI*, edited by John Brockman, 64–75. New York: Penguin Press, 2019.

Winograd, Terry. 'Artificial Intelligence and Language Comprehension'. In *Artificial Intelligence and Language Comprehension*, 3–25. Washington, DC: National Institute of Education, 1976.

Winograd, Terry. "LLM has a representation of care, it doesn't care. An interview with Terry Winograd by Harry Halpin," *Technophany Commentaries* (2025), https://philotechne.substack.com/p/commentaries-llm-has-a-representation

Wolfram, Stephen. *What Is ChatGPT Doing ... and Why Does It Work?* Champaign, IL: Wolfram Media, 2023.

WSJ. 'Greenspan Testimony on Sources of Financial Crisis'. *The Wall Street Journal*, 23 October 2008. https://www.wsj.com/articles/BL-REB-2187.

Ypi, Lea. *The Architectonic of Reason. Purposiveness and Systematic Unity in Kant's Critique of Pure Reason*. Oxford: Oxford University Press, 2022.

Yudkowsky, Eliezer. 'Pausing AI Developments Isn't Enough. We Need to Shut it All Down'. *Time Magazine*, March 2023. https://time.com/6266923/ai-eliezer-yudkowsky-open-letter-not-enough/.

Zammito, John. 'Kant's Persistent Ambivalence toward Epigenesis, 1764–90'. In *Understanding Purpose: Kant and the Philosophy of Biology*, edited by Philippe Huneman, 51–74. Suffolk: Boydell & Brewer, 2007.

Zammito, John. *The Genesis of Kant's Critique of Judgment*. Chicago, IL: The University of Chicago Press, 1992.

Index

Note: Page numbers followed by 'n' denotes note numbers

Abbé de Saint-Pierre 91, 99
Abelard, Peter 11 n.38
Absolute 12, 64, 93
accumulation 35–6, 70
aesthetics xii, 55–6, 104, 106
Agamben, Giorgio 46
Agre, Philip 34 n.107
AI systems 12, 35 n.110, 47, 75 n.2
  goals 45
  superintelligent 45
Aigner, Franziska x, xiii, 28 n.86
algorithm 14–15, 33–4, 36–7, 50, 53–4,
    60, 65, 67, 77–9, 82, 94, 96, 98,
    100–2, 104
  backpropagation 9
  optimization 34
  organic 100
  recommender 10
  recursive 37, 59, 100
  training 47
algorithmic information theory 36, 60, 67
alignment 34, 45–6, 48–50, 67
  super 49–50
Allison, Henry E. 16 n.48, 17 n.50, 69
    n.82, 89 n.37, 96 n.63
Altman, Sam 50
analogy 2 n.7, 4, 22, 54–7, 67, 73, 85
anamnesis 49
Anderson, Chris 37
anthropology 59 n.53
antinomies 15, 19, 27, 43 n.11, 56 n.42,
    62–3, 83–4
Apel, Karl-Otto 94
apperception 23
architectonic 26 n.77, 28–31, 71
  of Pure Reason 71
  unity 26 n.77, 28–31, 71
architektonikê 28

Arendt, Hannah 71 n.91, 83 n.16, 98
    n.72, 100 n.77
Ariadne's thread x
Aristotelian ethics 72
Aristotelian hylomorphism 4
Aristotle 11, 21 n.66, 46, 70–1, 79 n.8
  Eudaimonia 72
  On Interpretation 11 n.38
  Magna Moralia 70–1 n.90
artificial general intelligence (AGI) 6,
    46–7, 75–7, 87
artificial intelligence (AI) x–xi, xiii, 1–3,
    5–10, 13, 27, 33–40, 45–50, 53,
    66–7, 75–9, 103–4
  apocalypse 49
  current 2–3, 5, 11, 16, 20, 32–3,
    46, 59
  ethics 45, 76
  for peace 78
  scientists 3, 34, 46, 48
  slowdown 46
  symbolic 5, 8
  warfare competition 103
  weapons 103
AI. *See* artificial intelligence
Artificial Life 1 n.1, 39 n.1
artificial organs 23 n.71, 74 n.96, 82
Asimov, Isaac 45–6
associations 9–12, 33, 35
  rules of 10, 19
atomic bomb 47, 103
atomism 69
  logical 6
automata xii, 33, 38, 44, 77, 106
automation xii, 32, 46, 59, 68, 75
autonomy xii, 15, 20, 25, 28, 42–3, 59,
    68–9, 84
Azuma, Hiroki 102 n.81

Index

Baumgarten, Alexander   27, 55–6
Bayes, Thomas   12–13, 37
beautiful   29, 41, 54–7, 61, 67, 89
Benanti, Paolo   75–6
Bengio, Yushua   xi, 9 n.31, 37 n.118
Bergson, Henri   32, 74 n.96
Bergsonian time   32
Bible   88, 92
Blumenbach, Johann Friedrich   xn7, 21, 21 n.62, 25
Boethius   11 n.38
Boltzmann machines   35
Brooks, Rodney   34 n.107
businessmen   87–8, 92

Cambrian Intelligence   34 n.107
Canguilhem, Georges   74 n.96, 82
Cantwell Smith, Brian   34 n.107, 35 n.110
capital   52, 70–1
   accumulation   104
capitalism   70–1, 94–5
Cassirer, Ernst   xii, 14, 87 n.27
categories   11 n.38, 15, 18–20, 23–4, 31, 35, 59, 61, 62 n.61, 96, 98. *See also* transcendental categories
categorical imperative   43–4, 53–4, 57 n.48, 59–60, 64, 72, 92–4
causality   9–11, 19, 30, 43–4, 69, 72, 83
   linear   5, 30, 32, 44, 70
   non-linear   69, 83
Caygill, Howard   xiii, 63 n.66, 96 n.63, 104
   Art of Judgment   63 n.66, 96 n.63
   On Resistance   104
Chaitin, Gregory   60 n.56, 67
Chalmers, David   2 n.9
Chiang, Ted   37
China   14, 91, 97, 102–3
Chinese philosophy   81
Church, Alonzo   61
Clausewitz, Carl von   104
cognition   9 n.33, 15 n.45, 17, 41 n.6, 61, 63, 89
   faculty of   18, 45, 60–1, 66
   ground of   23, 81
Cohen, Hermann   ix
commerce   94–6, 101 n.78
community   82–3, 95–9, 101–2. *See also* reciprocity

computable   37, 60, 66, 66 n.75
concept   ix–x, xii, 7, 9–12, 14–18, 20–1, 23–5, 28–30, 42–3, 45 n.16, 55–6, 63, 65–6, 69, 80, 83, 95–6, 99, 102 n.81
   affirmative   85
   dynamic   ix
   empirical   18, 23 n.70
   negative   84–5
   pure   18, 23–4
   transcendental   23, 56 n.42
connectionism   8–9, 34–5
constitution   17 n.50, 21 n.62, 93, 106
   perfect state   98 n.74
   republican   94
contingency   10, 12, 17, 20, 24, 29, 33, 52–3, 59, 68–9, 90, 102 n.81
cosmopolitan   85 n.20, 93–5, 98, 106
cosmos   65, 73, 81
critical philosophy   ix, xi, 35, 58, 82, 89–90, 99, 105, 107
criticism   viii, xii, 16. *See also* dogmatism
cyberneticians   28, 33 n.103
cybernetics   x–xi, 15, 28, 32–3, 40, 44–5, 105–7
   development of   xi, 32

Dartmouth Artificial Intelligence Conference   3, 8 n.28, 27 n.83, 36
Darwin, Charles   19, 23, 25
DeepSeek   103
Deleuze, Gilles   11, 54 n.33
Derrida, Jacques   8 n.25
Descartes René   4–8, 16 n.49, 18, 20–1, 32
   Cartesian machine   2, 4–5, 7, 10, 18, 38
   demon   4
   'Description of the Human Body'   4
   Discourse on the Method   4 n.14, 16 n.49
deus ex machina   93
Diagne, Souleymane Bachir   93 n.53
disposable time   70–1
dogmatism   xii   16–17, 24, 27, 107
Dreyfus, Hubert   5–9, 33–5
   Skillful Coping: Essays on the Phenomenology of Everyday Perception and Action   5 n.18, 7 n.24, 8 n.27

What Computers Cannot Do: Critique of Artificial Reason 6 n.20
Dreyfus, Stuart 7
Dupuy, Jean-Pierre 19 n.55, 33 n.103

ecclesiastics 90, 92
Egyptian God Theuth 49
electroencephalography 13
electromagnetism xin11
embryology 21, 24
emotion 14, 39, 87, 89
empirical
  laws 84
  norms 67
empiricism 2–3, 9–10, 13–17, 20–1, 23–4, 30, 35–7, 41–5, 51–4, 57–9, 63–6, 80, 86, 90, 93, 96–7, 106
energy 34
  dissipation of xi n.11, 68, 73
end of history 72, 100
end of nature 45 n.15, 68, 72–3
entropy 68, 73–4. *See also* energy, dissipation of
Entscheidungsproblem 60
environment 33, 73, 76–7
epigenesist ix 20–5, 27, 62, 106
  of pure reason ix, xiii, 20, 23–4, 41, 62, 65, 105
epistemological shift 105
epistemology xi, 5, 33, 37, 81–2, 88
equilibrium 98–100
eros 49
Erweiterung. See expansion
ethics 19 n.55, 45, 53 n.32, 71–2, 76, 86
Europe 48, 80, 91 n.42, 99, 101
Evans, Richard 19 n.55, 35 n.111
evil 41–2, 51, 58, 93 n.56
evolution viii, 1, 23, 24 n.72, 25
Ex Machina 49
exchange 85, 97, 101–2
existence 1, 3–4, 15 n.46, 46, 61, 63–9, 74, 83–4, 105
expansion 19, 23–4, 44
  of reason 19, 23, 44, 62–4, 106
experience 2–3, 9, 12, 16–20, 22–4, 26, 36 n.113, 41 n.6, 45 n.15, 51, 53, 58, 61, 82–3, 102
  aesthetic 61

condition of 24
subjective 81

faculties 2, 15–17, 27, 31 n.96, 45, 55–6, 59–62, 71 n.90, 86–7, 89–90, 105
  of cognition 18, 45, 60–1, 66
  cognitive 15, 23 n.71
  of desire 15, 45, 55, 59–60, 62, 89–90, 105
  of feeling 15, 55, 60, 62, 89
  higher 86–7
  theology 92
  transcendental xii, 17 n.50, 18 n.54, 20, 24, 37
Fenves, Peter 41 n.6
Fichte, J. G. 101–2, 104
Foucault, Michel 48
Free Energy Principle 34
freedom xii, 29, 41–5, 55, 58–9, 63–6, 69 n.81, 69 n.85, 82, 88, 90–1, 93
Freeman, Walter 8 n.26, 75 n.1

Garve, Christian 27 n.81, 65 n.73
Gegenstand 6
genealogy 50, 74 n.96
geography 86
geology 22–3, 35, 62, 79
geometrical axioms 96 n.63
geometry 4, 67 n.77, 69, 85–6, 96
God 16, 19, 49–50, 63–7, 69, 82
Gödel, Kurt xi, 33, 61
  Incompleteness Theorem 60
Gödel Machines 33 n.104
Goethe, Johann Wolfgang von 89 n.37
governance 77
  planetary 49, 77, 79, 102
GPU 9, 47
Greenspan, Alan 52–3
Grotius, Hugo 91, 94, 98
Guyer, Paul 48 n.23

Habermas, Jürgen 94 n.60
Halpin, Harry 8 n.25
Hanseatic League 103
harmony 27, 55–6, 82–3, 85, 93, 96 n.63, 98, 100
Haugland, John 5, 66
Hayek, Friedrich 98 n.71, 104–5
Hegel, G. W. F. 42, 81–2, 104

Heidegger, Martin   5–9, 31 n.97, 34, 58 n.52
   Being and Time   7–8
   Schelling's Treatise on the Essence of Human Freedom   31 n.97, 58 n.52
   Vorhandenheit   5
   Zuhandenheit   6
Heideggerian AI   8–9
Henrich, Dieter   15 n.45, 53 n.32
Herder, Johann Gottfried von   ix n.6, 22, 55 n.37, 68
heuristic   54, 58, 83, 85, 106
   searching   104
   speculative   97
highest Good   54, 63, 65–6, 71–2, 99–100, 105
Hilbert, David   60 n.55
Hinton, Geoffrey   xi, 8 n.38, 35 n.11, 37 n.118, 46
Hobbes, Thomas   53 n.32, 85, 98
homo deus   50, 76, 87
homo sapiens   76
Hui, Yuk xiii, 5 n.15, 11 n.37, 32 n.100, 33 n.104, 45 n.16, 56 n.40, 64 n.69, 69 n.85, 74 n.96, 76 n.4, 82 n.14, 96 n.64, 98 n.71, 107 n.90
   Art and Cosmotechnics   xii, 56 n.40, 64 n.69, 64 n.70, 105 n.86
   On the Existence of Digital Objects   11 n.37
   Machine and Sovereignty   xii, 74 n.96, 76 n.4, 82, 98 n.71, 105 n.86
   Recursivity and Contingency   xii, 5 n.15, 32–3, 45 n.16, 69 n.85, 74 n.96, 82–3, 96 n.64, 105 n.86
human subject   16–17, 82
humanity   43, 72, 76, 80, 86, 98 n.74, 103, 106–7
humans   xii   3, 14, 19, 27, 39–41, 44–6, 48, 53, 66, 73, 75, 77, 80–1, 88–9, 99, 103, 105–6
Hume, David   10 n.35, 11–12, 27 n.81, 35, 51, 53 n.32, 100–1, 107 n.89
   Essays, Moral, Political, and Literary   101 n.78
   trade, jealousy of   100–1
   A Treatise of Human Nature   10 n.35, 11, 51 n.27, 51 n.28, 51 n.29, 51 n.30

Hume machine   9 n.34, 35
Humean
   associationism   10–11
   epistemology   37
   moral machine   51–2, 58
   scepticism   53
Humean machine   2, 9–10, 18, 35, 38, 52, 54, 59
Huneman, Philippe   ix   20–1
Husserl, Edmund   6
Hutcheson, Francis   53 n.32
hylozoism   68
hypomnesis   49

IBM   76
idealism   68–9, 102, 107
ideas
   rational   56, 82
   regulative   45 n.15
Illetterati, Luca   29 n.89, 31 n.95
imagination   xi   10, 18, 23 n.71, 29, 55–6, 61, 106
imitation game   61
immortal Soul   34, 63–6, 82
imperatives   43 n.11, 56, 60. *See also* categorical imperative
   hypothetical   43, 56
   technical   56
impossible   12
improbable   12
incomputable   60–1, 66
individuation   xin11, 11 n.38, 63–4, 100
induction   20, 22 n.69, 36
intelligence   xii, 1–3, 5–6, 8–9, 13, 15–16, 18–20, 22, 27, 46–7, 75, 77, 105
   nature of   5–6
intelligent machine   xi, 1–37
Intelligenz   15
intelligere   9 n.33, 15
internal purposiveness   29–31, 68
international trade   xii, 94, 96–8, 100–1
intuition   18, 23 n.71, 44 n.14, 55
   intellectual   26
   sensible   26
invention   xiii, 25 n.73, 45 n.15, 47, 83 n.17, 90
invisible hand   101
irrational   3, 64, 81

Jacobi, Friedrich Heinrich   69 n.85
James, William   63 n.64
Japanese philosophy   81
Jefferson, Geoffrey   39
Jesus   50
judgement   11 n.40, 17, 22 n.69, 24,
    29–31, 53, 55–7, 61, 63–4, 67,
    69, 83–4, 91 n.42, 106
  aesthetic   54, 85
  analytic   18
  antinomy of   25, 83
  aporia of   63 n.66
  determinative   31, 56 n.42, 83–4
  mathematical   19
  power of   22 n.69, 31–2, 54
  reflective   96 n.63, 100 n.77, 104 n.83
  synthetic   17, 24

Kandinsky, Wassily   67–8
Kant, Immanuel   ix–xiii, 9 n.33, 15–33,
    35, 37, 41–5, 49, 53–66, 68–9,
    71–4, 81–107
  aesthetic judgment   100 n.77
  *Anthropology from a Pragmatic Point of
    View*   59 n.53
  Conflict of the Faculties   81 n.12,
    86–9, 92
  Critique of Judgment   ix, xi, 17 n.50,
    21, 24–5, 27 n.82, 29–33, 44–5,
    54–7, 61, 63 n.66, 64 n.68, 68
    n.78, 69 n.80, 69 n.81, 69 n.84,
    69 n.86, 72 n.92, 83–4, 87, 96
    n.63, 100 n.77
  Critique of Practical Reason   ixn6,
    27, 29, 31 n.97, 41, 43–4, 54, 59
    n.53, 63 n.65, 66 n.74
  Critique of Pure Reason   15, 17–21,
    23–6, 28 n.86, 29 n.87, 29 n.88,
    30 n.91, 31 n.96, 31 n.97, 34, 43
    n.9, 45 n.16, 62 n.60, 65 n.72, 90
    n.40, 96
  'Critique of Teleological
    Judgment'   33 n.103
  *Dreams of a spirit-seer elucidated by
    Dreams of Metaphysics*, ixn4, 26
  'Gefühl'   106
  *Groundwork of the Metaphysics of
    Morals*   42–3, 59 n.53, 85–6,
    91–3, 95–6, 105–6

  'as if' (*see* mode of 'as if')
  Inaugural Dissertation   ix   26
  Jäsche Logic   9 n.33, 22 n.69
  Kant's algorithm   97, 99, 105
  Kant's categories   11 n.38, 15,
    18–20, 23–5, 31, 35, 59, 61–2,
    81, 96
  Lectures on Logic   9 n.33, 15 n.47, 22
    n.69
  'On a Pure Mysticism in Religion'   81
    n.12, 92
  Opus Postumum   57 n.48, 73, 104
  Political Writings   ix, xii, 31 n.96, 86
    n.23, 88 n.31, 89 n.35, 91 n.45,
    97 n.69, 98 n.74, 100 n.77, 106
    n.88, 107 n.90
  *Prolegomena to Any Future
    Metaphysics*   27 n.81,
    41 n.5
  reflective judgement, ix   31, 33, 54–5,
    57–8, 69, 83–4, 90, 96, 104
  *Religion within the Boundaries of Mere
    Reason and Other Writings*   41,
    65 n.71
  teleological judgement   18, 29, 31
    n.95, 54, 71, 85
  'Toward Perpetual Peace'   ix, xii, 91
    n.46, 91 n.47, 94 n.58, 94 n.59,
    94 n.60, 95 n.61, 97 n.68, 98
    n.70, 98 n.72, 98 n.73, 100–1
  'Treaty of Perpetual Peace in
    Philosophy'   17 n.51, 83,
    89–90, 92 n.52, 93 n.54, 93 n.55,
    98, 102
  Vienna Logic   15 n.47
  'What is Enlightenment'   88
  Zweckmässigkeit ohne Zweck   29
Kantian   ix, 33, 35, 57, 74 n.96, 102
  algorithm   100
  antinomy   62
  epistemology   81
  freedom   43
  intelligence   16, 19
  machine   2–107
  moral machine   51, 58–9
  Moral Test   41
  morality   54, 58, 64
  peace machine   100, 105
  perpetual peace   100

Kant's
  System   x, 26, 57
  transcendental philosophy   15, 19 n.55, 54
Karatani, Kojin   102 n.81
King Friedrich Wilhelm II   86
Kleene, Stephen   61
Kleingeld, Pauline   95 n.61, 101 n.80
knowledge   ix, 2, 16, 26, 40, 42, 49, 61, 80, 82, 84, 90, 106
  historical   86
  rational   86
  sensible   55 n.39
Kojève, Alexandre   57, 72, 90
Königsberg   xii, 93, 103
Korsgaard, Christine   48 n.23
Kuehn, Manfred   59 n.53
Kuhn, Thomas   3, 59

Lambert, J. H.   ixn4, 26, 28 n.84
language   6, 16, 36, 63 n.63, 96
  pattern   10
  shared   76
Latour, Bruno   9 n.34
LeCun, Yann   xi, 2–3, 9 n.31, 13, 37 n.118, 46
Lehmann, Gerhard   x, 28 n.86, 54 n.35, 56–7, 73 n.94
  'Die Technik der Natur'   x, 28 n.86, 56–7
Leibniz, Gottfried Wilhelm   10, 15 n.45, 17 n.50, 22, 67, 69 n.83, 95–6
Leica camera   18 n.54
Lemmens, Pieter   xiii
Lenoir, Timothy   ix, 20–1, 25 n.75
Leroi-Gourhan, André   74 n.96
life   6, 30 n.93, 63 n.64, 65, 72–3, 76, 87–8
LLMs   8 n.25, 12, 34–8, 46–7, 50, 68, 76, 78, 103
Locke, John   17 n.50, 22, 66 n.76
Longo, Giuseppe   14
Lorenz, Konrad   18 n.54, 19, 24
Lovelace, Ada   1–2
Luhmann, Niklas   33
Lyotard, Jean-François   45 n.15, 63 n.66

McCarthy, John   xi, 27 n.83
machina sapiens   76–7

machine intelligence   1, 39, 52
machine learning   x   8, 34–5, 37
  algorithms   34–6
  pioneers of   37, 46
machines   x–xiii, 1–5, 10, 13–14, 16, 18, 20, 32–4, 37–41, 44–6, 48–9, 51–3, 58–61, 66–8, 70, 72–9, 81–2, 102–3, 105–6. *See also* Cartesian Machin; Hume Machine; Kant Machine
  computational   1 n.3, 9, 14, 40, 67
  cybernetic   32, 106–7
  empirical   2, 53, 67
  evil   41
  purposiveness of   70
Malabou, Catherine   21
Malaspina, Cecile   73 n.95
Malebranche, Nicolas   21 n.66
Marx, Karl   70–1
mathematics   14, 17, 20 n.59, 52, 67, 72, 83, 86
Maturana, Humberto   33
mechanical laws   83–4
Meillassoux, Quentin   81
metaphysics   xii, 7, 11 n.38, 17, 22, 26–9, 34, 65 n.72, 79, 84
Mill, John Stuart   70
Minsky, Marvin   xi, 5–6, 8, 27 n.83
mode of 'as if'   57–8, 64, 66, 68, 90, 97
mode of truth   57, 68, 97
monads   95–6
Montesquieu   95 n.61
moral
  law   42–5, 59, 61, 63 n.63, 66, 69, 73
  life   82, 92
  machine   xii, 39–73
  norms   45, 48, 50–2, 65
  order   48 n.23
  Turing test   41
morality   27, 29, 31, 41–3, 45, 50–1, 53–7, 59 n.53, 61–2, 65–8, 71–2, 74, 86, 94, 97, 100–1, 105
  organology of   74
  symbol of   54–5
moral-practical reason   44, 89, 92
Morris, William   70
Musk, Elon   50
nations   47, 77, 80, 95–6, 99–101
NATO   79

Index

natural sciences xi, 17, 22, 62, 86, 104
nature 18, 22, 24, 29–31, 40–5, 54–6, 64, 68–9, 71–4, 85–6, 90–2, 98–9, 103
  hidden plan of 98
  purposiveness of 68, 70–1, 73
  technics of x, 28 n.86, 56, 99
negentropy 73
negotium 71
Neiman, Susan 62 n.62
neural networks 8, 12 n.42, 14, 35, 40
neurodynamics 8 n.26
Newell, Allen xi, 2–3, 32, 34
Newton, Isaac 22, 83
Newtonian
  physics ix, xi 44, 73
  time (reversible) 32
Nietzsche, Friedrich 42, 50, 74 n.96, 93
nominalism 11 n.38, 66 n.76, 81
non-rational 64
norms 12, 42, 48–9, 52, 58, 66–7, 74, 79, 97
  moral 45, 50–2, 65
  social 48, 67
noumenon ixn4, 26–7, 56 n.40, 90
nuclear weapons 47, 52, 103–4

oneness 77, 79, 102
Open AI 15
Opium Wars 102
organic 77, 82, 105
  epistemology 82
  logic 30
  unity 26, 96
organicism ix, 21, 24–5, 30, 32, 45, 77, 82, 94, 96, 98 n.71, 105–6
organology 23 n.71, 74 n.96, 82, 106
organon 23 n.71
otium 71

pantheism 68–9
paradox 46, 79 n.8, 85
  of mechanization 5, 67
Parmenides 79 n.8
peace 75–6, 78–9, 83, 90–2, 94–5, 97–105, 107
  algorithm 83, 102
  machine 75–107
  treaty 77, 92–3

perpetual peace 79, 81–2, 91–2, 94–5, 97–100, 102–3, 105–6
  algorithm of xi, 75, 89, 101
Phaedrus 34, 49–50
Pharmakon 49
phenomena xi n.11, 7, 16–18, 26, 28, 37, 61, 67, 74, 80, 90
philosophy ix, xi–xiii, 1 n.1, 5–6, 11, 16–17, 19, 22, 28 n.84, 34, 38–9, 41, 59 n.53, 64 n.67, 65 n.73, 69, 71, 81, 86–7, 89–90, 92–3, 99 n.75, 103–4
  analytic xiii, 8
  contemporary 21 n.65, 35, 45
  continental 7
  history of, xi, xiii, 3, 6, 16, 32, 39, 45, 64
  moral 41, 53, 59 n.53
  political ix, 99
  speculative 27 n.81, 64 n.67
  transcendental 15–16, 58 n.51, 73
physics, laws of 72, 74, 83
planetary 47, 49, 77, 79, 84, 88, 102
plasticity 57, 62
Plato 6, 21 n.66, 34, 41, 50 n.25, 79 n.8
Pope Francis 75
Porphyry 11 n.38
postcolonialism 79, 81, 84, 93
practical reason 22 n.68, 42, 54, 59 n.53, 62–3, 71 n.90, 92–3, 106
pragmatism 63 n.64
predictions 12–13, 52, 79, 103
pre-emptive wars 79
preformation 21, 24
probabilities 10–15, 37 n.116, 66–7
  posteriori 37
  prior 12, 37
probability theory 37
Proudhon, Pierre-Joseph 80
Pufendorf, Samuel von 91, 94
purposiveness 29–31, 55, 68–70, 83 n.16
  external 29, 31 n.95, 68
  principle of 61, 96 n.63
  relative 68
  utilitarian 72
Putin, Vladimir 103–4

quantum mechanics 80

rational 64, 72
rational agents 65, 79

rationalism 3–5, 7, 9–10, 16–17, 21, 24, 35 n.111, 52–4, 69
realism 68, 81
reason ix–xiii, 5, 9–10, 15–17, 19–23, 26–32, 42–4, 48–9, 51–2, 54–6, 58, 60–3, 65–6, 69, 71–2, 74, 81, 83–4, 87–90, 92–3, 99–100, 104–7
  pure 19–20, 23–4, 27–8, 42, 45 n.16, 63, 66, 97–8, 106
reciprocity 96–9, 96 n.65. *See also* community
recursive function theory 37 n.117
recursive functions 33, 37 n.117
  partial 37 n.117
recursive heuristics 34
recursive movements 64
recursive operation 33, 58, 99
  algorithm's 65
recursivity 33 n.104, 34–5, 37, 40, 57, 95–6
reflective operation 57, 82, 100 n.77
regulative principle 25, 29, 31, 45 n.16, 58, 83, 96, 102, 104
relation 10–11, 11 n.38
  natural 11
  philosophical 11
  reciprocal 96
representation 6, 8 n.25, 18, 21, 55–6, 67
  categorical mental 34
  cognitive 5
  coherent mental 15
  formal logical 5
  symbolic 5
Revelation 37 n.117, 50 n.26
revolution xii, 17, 86–7, 91
  industrial 47, 73–4
  political 87
rights 78, 80, 85, 91–5, 98–9
robot revolts 46
robotics xi, 45–7, 49, 103
Rosenblatt, Frank 8
Rousseau, Jean-Jacques 28 n.84, 85, 91, 99

scepticism xii, 9, 17, 27, 39, 107
Schelling, F. W. J. 58 n.52, 69 n.85, 104
schema 20 n.60, 28 n.86
  logical xiii
  nonlogical xiii

schemata 23 n.70, 55
schematism 18
scheme 28, 30, 51 n.30
  cognitive 5–6
  non-mechanistic 29
Schlosser, Johann Georg 89 n.37, 90 n.41
Schmitt, Carl 80
scholê 71
Schwärmerei 26, 49, 107
Searle, John R. 40
  Chinese Room Experiment 39–40
Sejnowski, Terrence J. 8 n.28, 35 n.112
self-consciousness 44, 89
Sellars, Wilfrid 20 n.60
sensible ix, 11 n.40, 26–7, 55, 57, 90, 93, 96 n.63
Shannon, Claude 27 n.83
Simon, Herbert A. 34
Simondon, Gilbert x–xi 11 n.38, 33, 44, 57, 63, 73–4
slavery 46, 48, 51 n.27, 53
  ancient 46, 48
Smith, Adam 101
Solomonoff, Ray xi, 36–7, 60
sovereignty 71 n.90, 85, 102 n.81
speculative reason 27, 44, 63, 89
Spinoza, Baruch 19 n.55, 68–9
spontaneity 15, 21, 23–4, 44
statistical mechanics 32, 35 n.112
Stiegler, Bernard 23 n.71, 74 n.96
Strauss, Leo 71 n.91
subject 5–7, 20 n.61, 21 n.62, 23, 41, 74, 81, 105 n.85
sublime 29, 45 n.15, 61, 66, 100 n.77
substance 9–11, 69
superintelligence 14, 50, 77, 88, 90, 102–3
supersensible 22 n.68, 27, 56 n.42, 61–2, 90
Swedenborg, Emanuel 26
synthesis 15 n.45, 23 n.71
synthetic a posteriori 17–18
synthetic a priori judgements 17–20, 24, 42, 96 n.63
synthetic order 65 n.72
system 5, 9, 12, 20, 24–6, 28–32, 48, 51–2, 57–8, 63–4, 69 n.85, 73, 75 n.2, 77, 80–1, 90, 93, 97, 99–100
  autopoietic 99

biological 34
contemporary second-wave 35 n.110
financial 53
formal 60 n.55
mechanical 5, 30
open 20
technical 52-3
transcendental 58

tariffs 97
taste 56
technical-practical reason 56
technics x, 23 n.71, 28 n.86, 56
technics of judgement 56
technics of nature x, 28 n.86, 56, 99
Technik 56
technological acceleration 87
technological futurists 75
technological reason, critique of x
technology x-xi, xiii, 37, 45-7, 49, 64 n.70, 70, 76, 78, 84, 87, 102, 104
  communications 52
  contemporary xi, 102
Teilhard de Chardin, Pierre 76, 99
teleology x 25, 28-30, 32, 41, 57, 69, 72-3, 83, 94, 99, 104, 106
  intrasubjective 15 n.45
  political 94
telepathy 61-2
theology 57, 86, 88
theoretical reason 23, 25, 42, 44, 49, 57, 63-4, 93, 106
theoretical-speculative reason 63-4
thermodynamics xin11, 32, 72-4, 100
  second law of (*see* entropy)
thing-in-itself 65, 82, 90
totality 7 n.21, 37, 58 n.52, 69 n.85
trade 95-8, 100-2
  free 98 n.71
trade wars 101
trading 96-7, 100-2
  international 102, 104
transcendence 77-8, 85
transcendental 15-16, 20, 22, 24, 28 n.84, 35, 59, 97
  analytic 15, 25

categories 18-20, 35, 98
condition 20
deduction 20, 59
dialectic 15
transcendental empiricism 35
transcendental idealism 21
transcendental illusion 49, 72, 97
transcendental laws 59
transcendental principle 58 n.52, 92, 97
transcendentalism 16, 18, 23
transhumanist 87
trolley problem 58
Turing, Alan xi, 1-2, 8 n.26, 8 n.30, 13, 33 n.104, 39-41, 52, 60-2
Turing machine 33, 37 n.116, 37 n.117, 58, 60-1
Turing test 27, 39-41

übersinnlich. *See* supersensible
Unbedingte. *See* absolute
Understanding viii, 15-18, 23-4 26, 29, 31, 62, 81-4
unity 15, 23, 28, 61, 69, 93
  systematic ixn6, 31 n.96
  systemic 28
  technical 28
universal 20, 22 n.69, 30-1, 54, 57, 59, 64, 78-81, 83-6, 88, 93
Universal Declaration of Human Right 80
universal happiness 71-2, 74
universal laws 43, 83
  pregiven 44
universal norms 80, 82
universality 80, 84-5, 93 n.53
  pregiven 24
  unconditioned 88
utilitarianism 68, 71-2, 74
Utopias 70, 91, 105

Van Gogh, Vincent 67
Varela, Francisco 30, 33
Vattel, Emer de 91
Vaucanson, Jacques de xii, 44
Vaucansonian automaton 44, 58
Vermögen. *See* faculties
Verweisungszusammenhang 6-7
Von Neumann, John 33
Vuillemin, Jules ix

wars   74 n.96, 75, 79, 81–2, 85–6, 90–2,
    94–5, 98, 100–5, 107
  machines of   103
weapon of mass destruction (WMD)   79
Weatherby, Leif   21–3
Weber, Andreas   30
Weizenbaum, Joseph   75
Whitehead, Alfred North   64 n.67
Wiener, Norbert   xi, 32, 73
Wilczek, Frank   34 n.110
Winograd, Terry   6, 8, 34 n.107
Wolff, Casper   21
Wolff, Christian   21 n.62, 53–4, 60 n.57,
    91, 94

Wolfram, Stephen   36
Wollaston, William   53 n.32,
    60 n.57
Wood, Allen   48 n.23
world
  republic   91, 102 n.81
  sovereignty   90
  state   79, 91
  trade   94 n.60

Yudkowsky, Eliezer   46–7

Zammito, John   ix, 20–1, 68 n.79
Zeughaftigkeit (instrumentality)   6